AI in Business: 2019

Progress, Challenges and Setbacks

John P. Desmond

DEDICATION

For my wife Diane P. Desmond, my much better half who puts up with me and without whose support this book woujld not be possible.

Table of Contents

Acknowledgements
5

Chapter 1 - AI Starting to Work for Business
6

Chapter 2: AI and Business Strategy, AI and Org Charts   24

Chapter 3: Challenges for AI in Business
39

Chapter 4 - Education for AI
53

Chapter 5: Salaries, Jobs in AI
78

Chapter 6: AI and Ethics
88

Chapter 7: AI Self-Driving Cars
101

Chapter 8: AI in Canada -- Leadership Sets the Direction   122

Chapter 9: AI at Google
137

Chapter 10: AI at Amazon
150

Chapter 11: AI at Facebook
157

Chapter 12: AI at Microsoft
165

Chapter 13: Executive Interview: Kesha Williams, Chick-fil-A   171

Chapter 14: Executive Interview: Dany De Grave, Sanofi   181

Chapter 15: Executive Interview: Yoshua Bengio   191

Chapter 16: Executive Interview: Amir Bonifatemin   201

About the Author
214

ACKNOWLEDGEMENTS

This is to acknowledge the executives who agreed to be interviewed by AI Trends during the year, and to the many hard-working journalists and contributors writing about AI whose works are acknowledged in this book. Every effort is made to recognize the work of content originators who write the facts. A civil discourse and well-informed citizenry depends on them.

Chapter 1 - AI Starting to Work for Business

One million combinations was achievable using an electromechanical machine — the bombe, named after the Polish-designed bomba — which could be used to eliminate large numbers of candidate settings of the Enigma, the German cipher machine. Alan Turing's bombe was the primary tool used by British and American codebreakers to read Enigma traffic, with over 200 bombes in operation by the end of the war. Credit: US National Archives

AI in Business Sees Setbacks and Advances in 2018

Business is gaining real experience in efforts to use AI this year, experience that encompasses the fits and starts of any major technology shift and upheaval. The goal is always to achieve payback, and reaching the goal is a challenge.

These examples illustrate the maturing of AI. Any maturing cycle is marked by some setbacks.

Setback for Self-Driving Cars

Over $80 billion was invested in self-driving car technology between August 2014 and June 2017, investments in core technologies and applications, according to research by Cameron Kerry and Jack Karsten of the Brookings Institution.

These technologies include automated vehicle guidance and braking, lane-changing systems, the use of cameras and sensors for collision avoidance, the use of AI to analyze information in real time, the use of high-performance computing and deep learning systems to adapt to changing circumstances through detailed maps.

Light detection and ranging systems (LIDARs) and AI are critical to navigation and collision avoidance. With radar and light beams measuring the speed and distance of surrounding objects, and sensors placed all around the vehicle, the instruments are designed to keep the passengers safe and to avoid accidents.

Ride-sharing companies such as Uber are among companies investing heavily in self-driving cars, with the idea presumably that they will still have a role to play if the dream of self-driving cars is ever fulfilled and drivers are no longer needed.

However, the effort suffered a setback in March 2018 when an Uber autonomous vehicle undergoing testing in Arizona struck and killed a pedestrian walking across the road with a bike. Uber was ordered to suspend testing in Arizona. Several months later, Uber announced its self-driving car research in Arizona was ending. In July, Uber announced a cautious restart of self-driving car research would happen in Pittsburgh.

The National Traffic Safety Board issued a preliminary report in May on the Uber accident in Arizona that concluded that Uber's vehicle failed to brake in time to prevent the crash. A final report, in which the agency could assign blame and make recommendations, is expected in early 2019.

Walmart Adopts Azure for Cloud, Fate of HANA Uncertain

Walmart had been using HANA, the cloud platform from SAP, to process transaction records from its more than 11,000 stores. SAP enhanced its in-memory relational database with AI underpinnings in 2017. However in July 2018, Microsoft announced a five-year partnership with Walmart that included a combination of AI, cloud and Internet of Things (IoT) services.

As part of the deal, Walmart and Sam's Club will migrate their cloud computing to Azure, and Walmart will use Azure's IoT platform to track HVAC, refrigeration and other systems, according to an account in Venturebeat.

The promise of HANA was great, when it was announced in 2015 that Walmart had chosen it. In a report conducted by IDC and sponsored by SAP, 10 organizations that use HANA said they expected to realize an average five-year return on investment of 575%. They projected an average annual benefit of $19.27 million per organization using HANA, compared to an average investment of $2.41 million over five years. The names of the organizations surveyed were not disclosed.

What happened with HANA at Walmart? That's a story needing research. Efforts to get a comment from Walmart public relations and SAP public relations for this book were not successful.

Karenann Terrell was the CIO of Walmart for six years and four months, departing in March 2017. She is now the chief digital and technology officer for GSK, GlaxoSmithKline, the pharmaceutical company. Efforts to reach her for comment were not successful.

Did the HANA marketing get in front of the technical development? It wouldn't be the first time in the software industry.

Yet Walmart continues to apply AI to its core business processes. In an [account in AI Trends](#) in November, Vimal Suba writes from a conference he attended an account from Yazdi Balgi, SVP, Global Business Services and Emerging Technologies at Walmart.

Walmart has used automation capabilities like Robotic Process Automation (RPA) to help with everyday office tasks such as digitizing documents. RPA systems leverage rules-based automation with visual and scripted flowcharts to automate backend service processes.

Walmart's back office processes payroll for over 2.2 million employees. A small process improvement can turn into huge savings at this volume. They noticed that the bottlenecks are typically in inputs and exception handling. AI takes RPA to the next level to automate decision making to improve cases of exception handling. For Walmart, approximately 85% accuracy on AI algorithms serves as a trigger point to take automated decisions.

Additionally, the tasks now appear simple because there is data to prove the process efficacy. Yazdi gave an example of how the sales tax refunds and audit process was improved using AI and Big Data. Earlier, only a sample set of tax items where audited. The sampling resulted in a lot of audits from the government.

"AI helped to scan the universe of audits versus just the sampled ones," Yazdi said.

The full universe scan empowers relevant staff members to enhance their human judgement with machine-oriented quantitative and qualitative decision advice. Of, or in many cases with reasonable accuracy, default to machine decisions.

On a question about whether Walmart is using Blockchain or not, Yazdi's response was very revealing.

"Machine learning and Artificial Intelligence are highly underestimated. Blockchain is overestimated," he said.

IBM Downsizes Watson Health

Multiple press reports in May maintained that **IBM** laid off a substantial percentage of its **Watson Health** business units, with reports as high as 50 percent to 70 percent of that workforce.

IBM issued this statement: "IBM is continuing to reposition our team to align with our focus on the high-value segments of the IT market. We're not discussing specific numbers of employees affected, but it's a small percentage of our global Watson Health workforce, as we move to more technology-intensive offerings, simplified processes and automation to drive speed."

So what happened?

Watson Health got some bad news in February 2017, when the MD Anderson Cancer Center, part of the University of Texas, ended its implementation of IBM Watson. An internal audit showed the work cost MD Anderson more than $62 million and had not achieved any of its goals.

"IBM spun a story about how Watson could improve cancer treatment that was superficially plausible – there are thousands of research papers published every year and no doctor can read them all," said David Howard, a faculty member in the Department of Health Policy and Management at Emory University, quoted in a story in HealthNewsReview.org. "However, the problem is not that there is too much information, but rather there is too little. Only a handful of published articles are high-quality, randomized trials. In many cases, oncologists have to choose between drugs that have never been directly compared in a randomized trial."

Discussion ensued in the industry on the lessons to be learned from this experience. Writing in Medium, Jesus Rodriguez, chief scientist at Invector Lab, stated, "These type of failures should be expected in a new and challenging discipline like AI on which traditional corporate IT teams lack knowledge and expertise."

Rodriguez suggested the lessons to be learned included that data quality matters, that data integration is key, lean and continuous delivery is suggested, and regular model training and performance monitoring is needed. The Watson Health-Anderson Center collaboration had been going on for four years before problems were detected.

Market competition got in the way of Watson when when electronic health record giant Epic started to block access to patient databases that IBM needed to fulfill its contracts, according to an account in Becker's Health IT & CIO report, quoting reporting from STAT. Epic claimed IBM was infringing on its intellectual property by leveraging the patient databases.

Some ex-employees were quoted as saying IBM management underestimated the time it would take to bring terabytes of data into an environment, standardize it, curate it and then make hundreds of measurements against it.

The head of IBM Watson Health, Deborah DiSanzo, left her role in the fall and was replaced by John Kelly, senior vice president for Cognitive Solutions and IBM Research, who will step into DiSanzo's role in an acting capacity, according to an account in Healthcare Informations, quoting reporting by STAT. IBM's third quarter earning report showed revenue from cognitive offerings including Watson was down six percent from the previous year.

The experiences are a setback for Watson Health, however the units continues its effort to gather the patient data needed to train its AI systems, such as by recent partnerships with Atrius Health in the Boston area, and the Central New York Care Collaborative, a state-funded agency that works with some 2,000 healthcare providers.

The main lesson may have been that the timeline was unrealistic for Watson Health to deliver for MD

Anderson and other accounts, and the repercussions are still being felt. Still, as Stephen Kraus, a partner at VC firm Bessemer Venture Partners, focusing on AI startups, said in speaking of the potential benefit of AI in healthcare to MIT Technology Review, "It's for real."

These reality checks on the progress of AI go side by side with evidence of initial paybacks from AI investments. Here are some examples:

General Electric Using AI to Help Manage Power Plants

General Electric said it is using artificial intelligence to make thermal power plants "more dynamic" and able to quickly respond to changes in the supply-demand balance on the U.S. grid, according to a recent account in Forbes.

With increasing amounts of intermittent wind and solar power coming online, baseload power plants are required to ramp up in a matter of seconds when the wind doesn't blow or the sun doesn't shine.

"We need to adapt the thermal fleet to this new world, to allow it to still serve a purpose on the grid and help to incorporate more renewable energy," said Mary Cauwels, product marketing manager of application performance management at GE Renewable Digital. AI can be used to "adjust how the power plant equipment runs in real time to help achieve more efficiency, flexibility and capacity", she said.

The technology is particularly useful for utilities with mixed fleets of thermal power and renewable generation. GE is working with Invenergy, PSEG Inc and Exelon Corp to help improve the efficiency of their thermal power fleets in the U.S. and "better predict wear and tear on the machines," said Cauwels.

System operators will be less likely to curtail renewables if they know that thermal power generation can be ramped up quickly at times of supply shortfall, she said. At gas-fired power plants, GE has been able to get an additional 15 megawatts onto the grid in the space of a minute, by using machine intelligence and automation to increase the ramp rate of such assets.

GE is also using AI to predict failures ahead of time at wind and solar plants, and this can bring about significant savings for the customer. Using digital twins – a digital simulation of a real life asset – at wind parks can increase annual energy production by 3 to 5 percent, according to John LaFleche, senior director of data and analytics at GE Renewable Energy.

John Deere Now Owns AI-Driven Blue River Technology

In agriculture, John Deere in 2017 acquired Blue River Technology, which was using machine learning algorithms to allow robots peering through precision cameras to decide whether to spray a plant with pesticide.

"Blue River is advancing precision agriculture by moving farm management decisions from the field level to the plant level," stated Jorge Heraud, co-founder and CEO of Blue River Technology, in a press release. "We are using computer vision, robotics, and machine learning to help smart machines detect, identify, and make management decisions about every single plant in the field."

Deere invested $305 million to fully acquire Blue River Technology. The plan was to have the 60-person Blue River firm remain in Sunnyvale. AI Trends reached out to John Deere public relations to ask if customers benefited from the acquired Blue River Technology in 2018.

"In joining Blue River's machine learning capabilities and John Deere's expertise in manufacturing high-quality machinery and technology, farmers will be able to navigate thousands of weed varieties, manage fields at the plant level and gather intelligence that will continuously make their equipment more precise," said .Deanna Kovar, Director, Production & Precision Ag Marketing at John Deere, to AI Trends.

In other AI news at John Deere, the company in the spring of 2017 established a San Francisco Lab to advance new technologies in AI, machine learning and robotics. It also gives Deere a presence in Silicon Valley for prospective partnerships, Kovar said.

Also, in May 2017, John Deere launched the S700 combine harvester, which utilizes intelligent, connected capabilities for more efficient grain harvesting. The combine uses a number of sensors and smart ActiveVision™ cameras that use image processing, a form of machine learning, to understand how the performance of the machine has changed. Factors like the slope of the land or the humidity in the air can alter the performance of a combine significantly over the course of a day or even a harvest season. "These machines are now smart enough to realize these changes and automatically adjust settings to maintain the customer's optimal performance day in and day out," Kovar said.

AI Assisting Journalists to Generate Local News in UK

The Press Association (PA) and Urbs Media are conducting a trial in the UK of RADAR, for Reporters and Data and Robots, a system in which journalists work with AI search capabilities to generate local stories that otherwise would go uncovered.

PA is a national news agency operating for over 150 years; Urbs Media is a technology startup attempting to combine reporters and automation to generate local news.

In a six-month pilot stage, RADAR said it has published hundreds of local stories. In the second phase running until the end of August 2018, the news service will be available to all UK local newsrooms. It is capable of creating up to 30,000 local stories each month, the firm said.

The service received launch funding in 2017 from Google's Digital News Initiative (DNI) Innovation Fund – a €150m commitment from the company to stimulate and support innovation in digital journalism across Europe's news industry.

Over the summer months, RADAR's staff journalists were to identify, write and template an average of 15 stories each week from national datasets. Around 250 versions of each story will be generated for a weekly output of close to 4,000 localised pieces of content.

Gary Rogers, Editor-in-Chief of RADAR, said in a press release, "The launch of our distribution website is a big step forward for RADAR. It means that we can expand beyond the titles in our pilot phase and provide strong local news stories to any title across the UK. The site is easy to use, and we hope that publishers will find it a valuable asset in helping to serve their local readers."

Paul Gallagher, Digital Innovations Editor at Reach, a publisher, said in the press release, "It is very interesting to see how the content has developed and also to see how journalists respond to the idea of using copy generated by AI, or 'robot'."

He added, "Developing data journalism has been a key part of our strategy at Reach and we are trialing the RADAR service to see if it will provide a new way of finding stories that are important to our audiences."

AI Paying Dividends in Healthcare

AI can be found across the care continuum. For example, at the patient level, Mount Sinai Health System is using AI to discover comorbid conditions previously unidentified in diabetes patients, according to an account in Health Data Management. Robots are augmenting nursing care by assisting patients with mobility. At a large, national cancer center, AI has enabled a concierge service mobile app that provides intelligent interaction regarding quality-of-life needs, such as food and housing. Google AI is being employed to scan eyes for cardiovascular problems.

Many providers are looking at how AI can help support the business operations of healthcare. As a recent Advisory Report article stated, "AI works best when paired with humans." The goal is to use AI to create efficiencies across the continuum that not only help staff in their roles, but that also free clinicians, caregivers and office staff to focus on more value-added activities. Put to work, AI can help augment and automate human tasks and functions where appropriate. It can even offer advice.

One form of AI—chatbots—can essentially fill the role of an office assistant by automating many tasks. By searching mounting amounts of data, it can make recommendations 20 percent faster than a manual search. Because it is voice driven, and studies show that humans can speak and hear three to four times as many words per minute than they can type, staff can work faster.

Healthcare organizations are just beginning to unlock the potential of AI in healthcare. The possibilities are many; right now impressive results are being gained by supporting caregivers and staff to help them work better and smarter.

Gartner Predicts AI Will Generate $1.2 Trillion in Business Value in 2018

Here we have made an effort to cite specific examples of companies benefitting from AI in 2018. The examples are not so easy to find, with many companies seeing AI as providing a strategic advantage which must be closely guarded.

A lot is happening as evidenced by research from Gartner announced in April, projecting AI will generate $1.2 trillion in business value in 2018, a 70 percent increase from 2017, and forecasted to reach $3.9 trillion in 2022.

Gartner, as credible as any source in its business, assesses the total business value of AI across all the enterprise vertical sectors covered by Gartner. The firm identifies three different sources of AI business value: customer experience, new revenue, and cost reduction.

- Customer experience: The positive or negative effects on indirect cost. Customer

experience is a necessary precondition for widespread adoption of AI technology to both unlock its full potential and enable value.
- New revenue: Increasing sales of existing products and services, and/or creating new product or service opportunity beyond the existing situation.
- Cost reduction: Reduced costs incurred in producing and delivering those new or existing products and services.

"AI promises to be the most disruptive class of technologies during the next 10 years due to advances in computational power, volume, velocity and variety of data, as well as advances in deep neural networks (DNNs)," said John-David Lovelock, research vice president at Gartner, in a press release. "One of the biggest aggregate sources for AI-enhanced products and services acquired by enterprises between 2017 and 2022 will be niche solutions that address one need very well. Business executives will drive investment in these products, sourced from thousands of narrowly focused, specialist suppliers with specific AI-enhanced applications."

"In the early years of AI, customer experience (CX) is the primary source of derived business value, as organizations see value in using AI techniques to improve every customer interaction, with the goal of increasing customer growth and retention. CX is followed closely by cost reduction, as organizations look for ways to use AI to increase process efficiency to improve decision making and automate more tasks," said Mr. Lovelock. "However, in 2021, new revenue will become the dominant source, as companies uncover business value in using AI to increase sales of existing products and services, as well as to discover opportunities for new products and services. Thus, in the long run, the business value of AI will be about new revenue possibilities."

Virtual agents allow corporate organizations to reduce labor costs as they take over simple requests and tasks from a call center, help desk and other service human agents, while handing over the more complex questions to their human counterparts. They can also provide uplift to revenue, as in the case of robo advisors in financial services or upselling in call centers.

The promise of AI certainly remains high, and the early stage experience is proving to be valuable in the cases we hear about where it works. In the cases we hear about where the AI does not work, such as in the Uber pedestrian fatality, we realize the the risks of putting complete faith in technology.

(Author's note: I encourage readers to share with me their experiences in trying to implement AI technology in their organizations. From shared experience, we learn.)

Chapter 2: AI and Business Strategy, AI and Org Charts

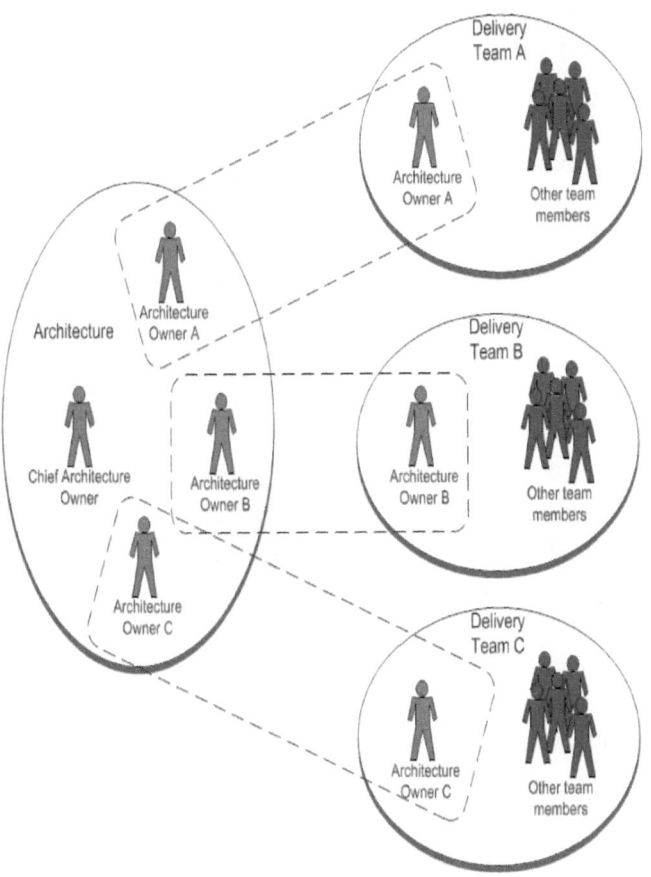

This agile enterprise team structure, with central expertise reaching out to other parts of the organization, can work for AI. Credit: The Disciplined Agile Consortium

As Business Deploys AI, "Work Architecture" Need a Redesign

Some 65% of children entering primary school today will have jobs that do not now exist, according to one estimate. To gain an understanding of what jobs are up and coming, and what skills are needed to succeed, LinkedIn studied data from five years to spot trends.

Among the key findings:

- Machine learning engineers, data scientists and big data engineers were among the top emerging jobs, with companies in a wide range of industries seeking those skills.
- Talent is scarce. Data Scientist roles have increases 650 percent since 2012, but currently in the US, 35,000 people are said to have data science skills. The supply of candidates for these roles cannot keep up with demand from the companies hiring.
- Many of the emerging needed skills did not exist five years ago; many professionals are not confident that their current skill set will still be relevant in one to two years.
- Software engineers are feeding into all the technology-related professions.

Here are some example strong growth titles from the LinkedIn study::

Machine Learning Engineer

1. Software Engineer

2. Research Assistant

3. Teaching Assistant

4. Data Scientist

5. System Engineer

Data Scientist

1. Research Assistant

2. Teaching Assistant

3. Software Engineer

4. Data Scientist

5. Business Analyst

Big Data Developer

1. Software Engineer

2. Hadoop Developer

3. System Engineer

4. Java Engineer

5. ETL Developer

AI is Seen Adding More Jobs Than Lost

The emergence of AI in the organization was seen to be adding more jobs than those lost by attendees at the EmTech Digital Conference from Ernst & Young and MIT Technology Review held in the spring of 2018.

While many companies are striving to implement AI on projects, few have tied AI into the overall business strategy. A basic notion is that AI will free people to do more interesting work.

Jeff Wong, EY Global Chief Innovation Officer, said in an article in MIT Technology Review, "As businesses deploy AI strategies, they're increasingly aware of how the roles, responsibilities and skills of their talent is changing. With AI taking a leading role on tackling organizations' simple and repetitive tasks, the human workforce can focus more on complex work that ultimately provides a greater level of professional fulfilment to employees and a more efficient use of critical thinking power."

Asked if AI is being used currently in their organizations, most respondents said AI is being piloted in one or more areas but there was no overall enterprise AI strategy. The next cluster reported that AI is currently not a strategic priority.

Chris Mazzei, EY Chief Data & Analytics Officer and Global Innovation Technologies Leader, stated, "While we're seeing momentum in businesses deploying AI more strategically across the enterprise, its application is often fragmented across business functions, leaving much of the potential untapped."

When asked for the top three desired business outcomes from the application of AI, the answers were: to improve and/or develop new products and services; achieve cost efficiencies and streamlined business operations, and to accelerate decision-making.

Chris Mazzei, EY Chief Data & Analytics Officer and Global Innovation Technologies Leader added: "AI technologies have been proven to streamline operations and speed-up internal processes. However, businesses should think more holistically about the competitive advantages that can be reaped from thoughtful applications of AI in product and service development, sales enablement, enhancing customer experience, or capturing business intelligence that helps impact the bottom line."

The talent shortage is holding things back. "Despite AI's potential to drive transformational change, adoption continues to be hampered by a shortage of talent," stated Nigel Duffy, EY Global Innovation Artificial Intelligence Leader. "Businesses must invest in and create a culture of continuous learning that comprises skills programs, training sessions, and research partnerships to attract and retain leading AI practitioners."

Businesses are aware they need to diversify their AI talent pools to try to prevent bias in results.

Jeff Wong stated, "There is a correlation between the continued lack of diverse AI talent and the distortions being found in some machine-learning outcomes. To mitigate this, businesses need to look for a wide variety of talent to ensure a diversity of experience, and social and professional perspectives are integrated at the coding stage."

AI on the March, with Humans in the Loop.

The 2018 Global Human Capital Trends report from Deloitte Insights found that the influx of AI, robotics, and automation into the workplace has dramatically accelerated in the last year, and "uniquely human" skills and roles were found to be critically important. Skills seen to be in high demand in the future included complex problem-solving (63 percent), cognitive abilities (55 percent), and social skills (52 percent).

Reinforcing this view, a recent World Economic Forum study found that the top 10 skills for the next decade include essential human skills such as critical thinking, creativity, and people management.

To maximize the potential value of these new technologies today and minimize the potential adverse impacts on the workforce, organizations must put "humans in the loop" —reconstructing work, retraining people, and rearranging the organization. The greatest opportunity is not just to redesign jobs or automate routine work, but to fundamentally rethink "work architecture" to benefit organizations, teams, and individuals.

The Deloitte study found a "readiness gap" with 72 percent of respondents seeing AI as important and 31 percent reported being ready to address it.

Leading companies are recognizing that the technologies are more effective when used to complement and not replace humans. Manufacturers including Airbus and Nissan are finding ways to use collaborative robots, or "cobots," that work side by side with workers in factories.

An algorithm is only as effective as "the quantity and quality of the training data to get [it] going," stated Lukas Biewald, CEO of CrowdFlower, a startup that provides algorithm trainers. This realization has given rise to new jobs with titles such as "bot trainer," "bot farmer," and "bot curator."

Tell the Humans They are Not Fired

As AI technology is introduced and deployed, the workforce needs new skills to be able to exploit the new technologies. "Work architecture" needs to be redesigned. Work needs to be decomposed into it fundamental components - for example production, problem-solving, communication, supervision - and ways that new combinations of humans and technology working together need to be defined.

Despite this recognition, the Deloitte study found companies are slow to develop the needed human skills of the future. Some 49 percent of respondents said they do not have a plan to cultivate them. "We see this as an urgent human capital challenge requiring top executive support to transform organizational structures, cultures, career options and performance management practices," the report stated.

Further, "Absent a thoughtful approach, organizations may not only risk failing to identify the skills they need to take effective advantage of technology, but also suffer damage to their employee and corporate brand due to perceptions around (real or supposed) workforce reductions."

The integration of early AI tools is also causing organizations to become more collaborative and team-oriented, to move away from traditional top-down hierarchical structures, according to an [account in Fast Company.](#).

"To integrate AI, you have to have an internal team of expert product people and engineers that know its application and are working very closely with the frontline teams that are actually delivering services," stated Ian Crosby, co founder and CEO of Bench, a digital bookkeeping provider. "When we are working AI into our frontline service, we don't go away to a dark room and come back after a year with our masterpiece. We work with our frontline bookkeepers day in, day out."

Org Charts Moving Away from Top-Down, Towards Teams

The Deloitte survey also found organizations are moving away from a top-down structure and toward multidisciplinary teams. Some 32% of respondents said they are redesigning their organizations to be more team-centric, optimizing them for adaptability and learning in preparation for technological disruption.

Finding a balanced team structure, however, doesn't happen overnight, Crosby suggested. In large organizations, "It's better to start with a small team first, and let them evolve and scale up, rather than try to introduce the whole company all at once."

Crosby adds that Bench's eagerness to integrate new technologies also determines the skills the company seeks in recruiting and hiring. Beyond checking the boxes of the job's technical requirements, he says the company looks for candidates that are ready to adapt to the changes that are coming.

"When you're working with AI, you're building things that nobody has ever built before, and nobody knows how that will look yet," he said. "If they're not open to being completely wrong, and having the humility to say they were wrong, we need to reevaluate."

Where to Start

When building something never built before, where does one start? "This is one of those instances where getting started is more important than where to start," suggests Trent Weier, a senior director with SAP who works with customers on projects, writing in Digitalist Magazine from SAP. "Building AI capabilities like machine learning is an evolutionary process and lends itself to short, focused discovery, design, prototyping, and delivery cycles."

SAP has found early use case experience for AI and machine learning have seen benefits in process optimization, demand planning and forecast applications. The forecast algorithm, for example, evaluates errors for each cycle and recommends or automatically adapts the forecasting method to produce the best result.

For inventory applications, machine learning can automatically adjust optimal safety stock values and inventory parameters at each echelon of the supply chain. Multi-echelon inventory optimization (MEIO) strives to maintain the optimal balance of components, work in process, and finished goods inventory.

AI Impact on Daily Work Environment

AI stands to change the daily work environment, suggests a recent article in MIT Sloan Management Review. "What people don't talk about is the integration problem. Even if you can develop the system to do very focused, individual tasks for what people are doing today, as long as you can't entirely remove the person from the process, you have a new problem that arises -- which is coordinating the work of, even communication between, people and these AI systems," stated Julie Shah, an associate professor of aeronautics at MIT. "And that interaction problem is still a very difficult problem for us, and it's currently unsolved."

The article is based on findings from the 2017 AI Global Executive Study and Research project conducted at MIT in partnership with Boston Consulting Group. The partners surveyed 3,000 business executives in the spring of 2017 from 112 countries and 21 industries, from organizations of various sizes, two-thirds of them outside the US.

While organizing for AI broadly, the enterprise will place a premium on soft skills and new forms of collaboration, including project teams composed of humans and machines.

Companies deploying AI are exploring many models of organization, with the Pioneers evenly split among centralized, distributed and hybrid organization models. The report suggests a hybrid model may make the most sense for large organizations, because companies need AI resources both centrally and locally. TIAA, for example, has an analytics center of excellence and a number of decentralized groups.

"The center of excellence is not intended to be the group that will provide all analytics for the entire organization. It provides expertise, guidance and direction to other internal teams that are working to deploy AI and analytics," said J.D. Elliott, director of enterprise data management for TIAA, a Fortune 100 financial services organization with nearly $1 trillion of assets under management.

The message is not having all the answers is not a reason to hold back from where AI will take your organization.
Role of Leadership

What is the role of leadership in the AI-driven organization? This is the question addressed by authors Thomas H. Davenport and Janet Foutty writing in August in MIT Sloan Management Review.

The authors suggest effective leaders of AI-driven organizations have seven attributes. Here is an edited summary:

They learn the technologies. Leaders outside of IT fields have not felt the need to understand technologies beyond the surface level, but AI is different. It is not just one technology, but many, each with its own application types stage of development, strengths and limitations. Leaders need to know enough about them to weigh in on which will be critical to their organization's success.

They establish clear business objectives. AI is capable of addressing virtually all the issues, but that's not realistic. Leaders need to make choices about where to deploy. The 2017 Deloitte State of Cognitive survey of US executives with a high level of AI awareness, found the most popular objectives involved using AI to improve existing products and services, make better decisions, create new products and optimize business processes. Senior managers need to make and own these decisions.

They set an appropriate level of ambition. If the moonshot project doesn't reach the moon, it might set back overall AI initiatives. The alternative is to undertake a series of less ambitious projects, the low-hanging fruit. In his 2017 letter to Amazon shareholders, CEO Jeff Bezos noted that while the company was undertaking some high ambitious projects, the bulk of its machine learning efforts were devoted to "quietly but meaningfully improving core operations." A series of such projects can add up to major change.

They look beyond pilots and proofs of concept. Leaders need to push their companies to scale up pilot projects to full production status. Best to identify process improvements before applying technology, and figuring out now to integrate AI technologies with existing applications and IT architectures. Not easy. AI-driven leaders must help assess the potential for full-scale implementation before embarking on pilot projects.

They prepare people for the journey. Most AI projects will involve "augmentation" - smart people working in collaboration with smart machines - rather than large-scale automation. Thus employees will need to learn new skills and adopt new roles. Good leaders are preparing their people by developing training programs, recruiting for new skills when necessary and integrating continuous learning into their models. This is starting to happen. Bank of America's Technology and Operations function developed a series of online education programs for over 90,000 employees that address some of the skills needed for work alongside the bank's chatbot "Erica" and other AI applications.

They get the necessary data. AI-driven leaders know that data is their most important asset if they want to do substantial work in AI. Leaders planning to use machine learning to predict what their customers will buy need high-quality data on what customers have bought in the past. Leaders of healthcare organizations that want to use deep-learning models to analyze medical images need a lot of images with labeled outcomes from which the system can learn. Many organizations will need to turn to external data to supplement their internal sources, and others will need to improve data quality and integration before they can use it with their AI projects.

They orchestrate collaborative organizations. Top executives - CEOs, heads of IT, operations, marketing and so on - are not known for collaborating closely on initiatives involving technology. But these groups need to work together in AI-driven organizations to set priorities, determine implications of technology architectures for needed human skills, and assess the implications for key functions. Deloitte has referred to this approach as "symphonic leadership," with players working in concert like an orchestra. These teams will enable progress in AI and communicate to the organization that a new way of working together and managing is being adopted.

(Author's Note: I encourage readers to share with me experiences of how AI work is organized in your company.)

Chapter 3: Challenges for AI in Business

Power house mechanic working on steam pump.1920, Lewis Hines.
National Archives and Records Administration, Records of the Work Projects Administration
(69-RH-4L-2)

Bias in AI Increasingly Recognized; Progress Being Made

Bias in AI decision-making and in the algorithms of machine learning, has been outed as a real issue in the march of AI progress. Here is an update on where we are and efforts being made to recognize bias and counteract it, including a discussion of selected AI startups.

AI reflects the bias of its creators, notes Will Byrne, CEO of Groundswell in [a recent article in Fast Company](). Societal bias - the attribution of individuals or groups with distinct traits without any data to back it up - is a stubborn problem. AI has the potential to make it worse.

"The footprint of machine intelligence on critical decisions is often invisible, humming quietly beneath the surface," he writes. AI is driving decision-making on loan-worthiness, medical diagnosis, job candidates, parole determination, criminal punishment and educator performance.

How will AI be fair and inclusive? How will it engage and support the marginalized and most vulnerable in society?

Courts across the US are using a software tool suspected to be biased against African-Americans, predicting future crimes at twice the rate of white people, and underestimating future crimes among white people, according to a recent report by ProPublica, the non-profit investigative journalism outfit. The software tool, developed by Northpointe, uses 137 questions including "was one of your parents ever sent to prison?" The tool is in widespread use; Northpoint has refused to make the algorithm transparent, citing its proprietary business value.

AI is only as effective as the data it is trained on, Byrne wrote in Fast Company. When Microsoft introduced Tay.ai to the world in 2016, the conversational chatbot was to use live interactions on Twitter to get "smarter" in real time. But Tay became horribly racist and misogynist and was shut down after 16 hours.

Trend Toward More Openness

Interest is high in how to open up the black box of AI decision-making algorithms. The **AI Now Institute** nonprofit is advocating for fair algorithms; they have proposed that if an algorithm providing services for people cannot explain its decision, it should not be used. Regulations requiring such transparency from AI systems are likely to be required in the near future. The General Data Protection Regulation standards of the European Union, which went into effect on May 25, 2018, pushes in this direction as well.

Within the data science community, **OpenAI** is a nonprofit developing open source code in the new field of explainable AI, focusing on systems that can explain the reasoning of their decisions to human users.

Some point to the importance of having teams with diverse backgrounds across race, gender, culture and socioeconomic background designing and building AI systems. The Ph.D. technologists and mathematicians who have advanced the AI field needs to expand. Sociologists, ethicists, psychologists and humanities experts need to join the ranks.

It may be that separate algorithms are needed for different groups. In job candidate software, predictors of successful women engineers and male engineers are not the same. Digital affirmative action may be able to correct for structural bias that might be invisible.

Efforts Underway to Address Bias in AI Include Startups

AI Now was launched at a conference at MIT in July 2017. The founders were Kate Crawford, a researcher at Microsoft, and Meredith Whittaker, a researcher at Google. In an email to MIT Technology Review, Crawford said, "It's still early days for understanding algorithmic bias. Just this year we've seen more systems that have issues, and these are just the ones that have been investigated.".

Cathy O'Neil is a mathematician and author of the book, "Weapons of Math Destruction," which highlights the risk of algorithmic bias. "Algorithms replace human processes, but they are not held to the same standards," she has said. "People trust them too much."

O'Neil is now head of Online Risk Consulting & Algorithmic Auditing, a startup set up to help businesses identify and correct bias in the algorithms they use. The firm's clients include Rentlogic, a company that grades apartments in New York City. The company is also engaged in several projects in industries such as manufacturing, banking and education.

Asked in an email interview with AI Trends about the outlook for addressing bias in AI algorithms, O'Neil said, "It's an emerging field. I'm not sure how or exactly when but within the next two decades we will either have solved the problem of algorithmic accountability or we will have submitted our free will to stupid and flawed machines. I know which future I'd prefer."

Also, "There's increasing academic work on the topic (see FAT* conference discussion below) but of course the IP laws and licenses tilt the playing field towards the tech giants. Not to mention that they are the ones who own all our data. So there's a limited amount that outside researchers can accomplish without regulations or subpoenas."

O'Neil continued, "But again I think the current state of affairs will end. I just don't know exactly how much damage will take place before it does."

FAT* Conference Gaining Steam

The conference on Fairness, Accountability, and Transparency (FAT*), which held its fifth annual event in February 2018, brings together researchers and practitioners interested in fairness, accountability and transparency in socio-technical systems.

This community sees progress being made to address bias in AI technologies and automated decision-making. The group has a multidisciplinary and computer science-focused perspective, said Joshua Kroll, program chair, in an email interview with AI Trends. "We've seen truly exponential growth in the interest in this area," said Kroll, a computer scientist who is a Postdoctoral Research Scholar at the UC Berkeley School of Information.

"From our early workshops on Fairness, Accountability, and Transparency in Machine Learning (FAT/ML) starting in 2014 with a few dozen people, we've had yearly doubling in both the amount of contributed work and the number of event attendees. At this year's conference, for example, we had over 500 people registered with a waiting list of over 400 people. And we've reached the selectivity of top-tier research venues in computer science to select the 17 research papers chosen for presentation as well as the six tutorial sessions," Kroll said.

He added, "One important improvement is the way scholars and practitioners alike are starting to view these problems as cutting across different concerns and requiring solutions from many disciplines. The community, by and large, realizes that there will be no single "most fair" algorithm, but rather that fairness (or the elimination of bias) will be a process combining measurements and mitigations at the technical level with improvements in human-level processes for understanding what technology is doing."

This year's FAT* featured an interdisciplinary group of speakers on a range of topics, including how to deploy responsible models in life-critical situations. One session focused on the use of machine learning to support screening of referrals to a child protection agency in Pennsylvania.

Presentations on face recognition systems showed that while they have very good performance overall (88-93% accuracy), they had much worse performance for darker-skinned faces (77-87% accuracy), and women (79-89% accuracy). Performance was even worse for people in the intersection of those two subgroups (i.e., darker-skinned females) (65-79% accuracy), Kroll said.

"Nearly all of the work at FAT* is meant to change the way people design and build these systems to help them understand and avoid problems of bias or other unintended consequences," he said. "The work on face recognition accuracy, for example, caused one of the companies whose systems were examined to replicate the study internally and make changes to their algorithms to reduce or eliminate the problem." The effect of those changes were not yet validated at the time of the conference.

"I think the most important takeaway from FAT* and the growth of this community has been the idea that we won't make algorithms fair, accountable, or transparent if we only think about how to intervene purely at the technical level," Kroll said. "That is, while it's important and useful to develop technologies that explicitly mitigate bias, we still need to understand which biases need to be corrected or which parts of a population need extra protection. And even when we know that, such as when the law forbids discrimination on the basis of a protected attribute like race or gender, we still need to take a wide view to understand the ways in which a system causes negative impacts to those protected groups."

Finally, he said, "It's exciting to me that we're starting to see ideas from this research community make the jump from the academic world into real practice. I'm excited to see companies thinking hard about these issues and sending top engineering leadership to engage with and learn from the research community on these problems."

(For more information, go to FAT.)*

Google Sensitized to Bias

Google's cloud-based machine learning systems aim to make AI more accessible; with that comes risk that bias will creep in.

John Giannandrea, AI chief at Google, was quoted in an October 2017 article in MIT Technology review as being seriously concerned about bias in AI algorithms. "If we give these systems biased data, they will be biased," he stated. "It's important that we be transparent about the training data that we are using, and are looking for hidden biases in it; otherwise, we are building biased systems. If someone is trying to sell you a black box system for medical decision support, and you don't know how it works or what data was used to train it, then I wouldn't trust it," he stated.

Google recently organized its own conference on the relationship between humans and AI systems, that included speakers on the subject of bias. Google researcher Maya Gupta described her efforts to make more transparent algorithms, as part of a project known internally as "GlassBox." A presentation on the difficulty of detecting bias in how Facebook selects articles for its News Feed was made by Karrie Karahalios, a professor of computer science at the University of Illinois.

Recruiting Software Firms Aim to Cut Down Bias

Recruiting software firms have a keen interest in reducing or eliminating bias in their approaches. **Mya Systems** of San Francisco, founded in 2012, does this through reliance on a chatbot named Mya. Co-founder Eyal Grayevsky told Wired in a recent interview that Mya is programmed to interview and evaluate job candidates by asking objective, performance-based questions, avoiding the subconscious judgements that a human may unconsciously make. "We're taking out bias from the process," he stated.

Startup **HireVue** seeks to eliminate bias from recruiting through the use of video- and text-based software. The program extracts up to 25,000 data points from video interviews. Customers include Intel, Vodafone, Unilever and Nike. The assessments are based on factors including facial expressions, vocabulary and abstract qualities such as candidate empathy. HireVue CTO Loren Larsen was quoted as saying that candidates are "getting the same shot regardless of gender, ethnicity, age, employment gaps or college attended."

The startup recruiting software suppliers are not blind to the possibility that bias can still occur in the AI system. Laura Matha, founder and CEO of AI recruitment platform **Talent Sonar** was quoted in Wired as seeing "a huge risk that using AI in the recruiting process is going to increase bias and not reduce it." This is because AI depends on a training set generated by a human team which may not be diverse enough.

This risk is echoed by Y-Vonne Hutchinson, the executive director of **ReadySet,** a diversity consultancy based in Oakland. "We try not to see AI as a panacea," she told Wired. "AI is a tool and AI has makers and sometimes AI can amplify the biases of its makers and the blind spots of its makers." Diversity training helps the human recruiters to spot the bias in themselves and others, she argues.

Figure Eight, Inc., formerly CloudFlower, is focused on training machine learning algorithms. Writing in AI Trends in March 2018, CEO Robin Bordoli argued that algorithmic bias is solvable. "We know that AI can both amplify existing bias and even evidence bias where none was intended. But it's solvable. It is. It's just a matter of being conscientious," Bordoli stated. "It means hiring smartly. It means testing smartly. And it means, above all, using the same data that makes AI work to make AI work more fairly."

Not so Fast on Explainable AI

Transparency in AI should be around the data powering the algorithms, suggests Rudina Seseri, founder of Glasswing Ventures, which invests in AI startups, writing in TechCrunch in June 2018. Companies should disclose where and how they got the data used to fuel the decision of the AI system. Consumers should own their data and be in control of the ways businesses use and sell such information, which is often done without clear consumer consent. Data is the foundation for all AI, so it is valid to want to know where it comes from and how it might explain biases.

Seseri suggests that "grandstanding by IBM and other tech giants around the idea of "explainable AI" is nothing but virtue signaling that has no basis in reality. I am not aware, for instance, of any place where IBM has laid bare the inner workings of Watson - how to these algorithms work? Why do they make the recommendations/predictions they do?"

Defining what is meant by explainable AI is a sticky wicket. It can quickly get quite complex, with a mix of algorithms, statistical models, changing parameters over time, cause and consequence relationships in the mix. What the models mean is unintelligible for most.

Then come the tradeoffs of truly explainable AI, such as performance and business risk. "If all the inner workings of an AI-powered platform were publicly available, then intellectual property as a differentiator is gone," Seseri states. Compelling a startup to explain exactly how a proprietary AI system works could be akin to asking that company to disclose its source code. "If the IP had any value, the company would be finished soon after it hit 'send,' she suggests. Thus, requirements that favor incumbents are likely to stifle innovations in startups.

FICO Working on Making AI More Explainable

One of the companies working on making AI more explainable is FICO, the San Jose, Calif.-based company best known for developing a patented credit scoring methodology, the "FICO score," used to determine credit risk. The launch of GDPR in Europe spurred FICO.

"A lot of our customers cannot really deploy machine learning algorithms in a lot of contexts," said FICO VP of Product and Technology Jari Koister, in an [article in Datanami,](#) a publication for data science professionals. If a deep learning system is to be used in fraud detection, for instance, it needs to be able to explain why. "It doesn't just have to do with regulation. It also has to do with just the confidence that when deployed, you can understand why the system is doing what it's doing," he said.

The FICO team has been working on its explainable AI project for two years. They initially worked with the University of California at Irvine on the LIME project, then decided to work on their own technique. The company rolled out their first release of what they call Explainable AI, at the FICO World Conference in April.

Feedback on the approach has been positive, with interest being shown by the Defense Advanced Research Projects Agency (DARPA), which last year launched its Explainable Artificial Intelligence (XAI) program. The two organizations are now sharing information.

Organizations that adopt FICO's Explainable AI will be able to generate "certificates of explanation," that provide insight into why the automated decision-making system generated its suggestion. "We're clearly at the cutting edge of opening up what is a black box to make it a white box," Koister sid. "And we're not done here. We're going to continue working on this. It's a very active area."

Chapter 4 - Education for AI

Women took over the jobs of men fighting overseas during World War I. Here these young women are delivering ice in 1918. Careers in AI today are open to anyone who can meet the qualifications.
Photo credit: National Archives.

Opportunities are Many

The opportunities are many for any young or mid-career person interested in working in AI. The education paths to become qualified to work in AI are also many, from the standard university degree path, to an online path that exploits many credible education resources for learning AI. Some suggest the quest to learn AI might result in a total transformation of higher education.

Here we use the experience of some real people to chart out the range of possibilities.

Yogesh Malik, FutureMonger - Advice for a Mid-Career Move into AI

Yogesh Malik, who calls himself FutureMonger, and describes himself as a "digital futurist" and "exponential thinker," recently wrote in Medium about how to reinvent yourself for a career in AI. When thinking about getting into AI, Malik suggests, "You need to go beyond your academic education, skills, and experience. While designing your career strategy—start with self-awareness, have a craftsman mindset, and seek out for short-term and long-term skills that need to be adopted or enhanced."

AI opportunities exist in every industry and also in ethics, philosophy, policy making, and civic planning. One approach for programmer types if to get your hands dirty learning machine learning and cognitive computing using a daily routine for months. Others may prefer a more formal education path, taking courses from Coursera, Edx or Udacity, and doing all the projects and assessments, then completing a few small projects. In that way, you can learn what you like, and what best relates to your area of expertise. You might also begin to see that AI is more than programming languages, tools and algorithms. It spans machine learning, deep learning, cognitive computing, neural networks, computer vision, natural language processing, language translation -- it is not limiting.

The two essential paths are formal education or self-learning. If you are already in a specific industry and want to build more relevant experience in the same industry then online learning is a great help. You could revamp your career by slowly and steadily gaining AI skills from various MooC (Massive Open Online Course) platforms like Coursera, Edx or Udacity.

If you are at the beginning of your career and this path is available to you, formal education from a top institution will provide a strong launching platform. You spend time with highly technical and creative people. If you work towards a Phd. in AI, you can contribute to the development of Artificial Intelligence. A lot will depend on the quality of your publications and your thesis, your letters of recommendations, and how effectively you can sell yourself.

For me personally, I started into Machine Learning with Andrew Ng's Machine Learning course on Coursera with absolutely no experience with AI, algorithms or programming. This course was created by Stanford University and taught by Andrew Ng, who was formerly the head of AI for Baidu AI Group/Google Brain. I was overwhelmed and highly discouraged.

Later I re-started with small online courses on Udemy, YouTube, and Lynda. They were helpful as their curriculum was mostly code-less. Later I dived into algorithms using Python and R without a proper understanding of coding, and then back to Andrew Ng's Machine Learning course and completed that. It took almost another year to learn specific machine learning stacks like Azure ML, TensorFlow, AWS Lex, AWS Polly, AWS Rekognition and AWS SageMaker.

If you have this opportunity to reinvent your career by learning Artificial Intelligence, it will be challenging but at the same time highly rewarding for your future career.

Kelly Peng, Data Scientist at Airbnb

This might be my favorite personal story of 2018, for its detail and straightforward honesty. It was published in July in Towards Data Science, a month after she started her job at Airbnb. Kelly Peng characterized herself as a weak candidate for a data science job when she started out, but she identified her weaknesses and worked to become better qualified. She offered these stats on her job search:

- Applications: 475
- Phone interviews: 50
- Finished data science take-home challenges: 9
- Onsite interviews: 8
- Offers: 2
- Time spent: 6 months

She earned a Bachelor's degree in Economics from a university in China and a Master's degree in Business Administration from the University of Illinois at Urbana-Champaign. After graduating, she worked as a data analyst for two years, with seven months as a contractor at Google, and another 16 months at a startup. She mostly wrote SQL queries, built dashboards, and give data-driven recommendations.

Not learning and growing to her satisfaction, she left her job and applied for the Galvanize Data Science Immersive program, a 12-week boot camp in San Francisco. She failed the statistics interview to enter the boot camp program for four times, then got admitted after passing the statistics interview on the fifth try.

The content taught at Galvanize was heavy on Python and machine learning, with an assumption the students have a strong foundation in statistic. Kelly struggled because she didn't know much about programming and was not strong in statistics. "I had no choice but to work really hard," she said. She did nothing but 12 hours of study every day, with no break, no entertainment, no dating, nothing else. She began to get comfortable with the courses in time.

She started interviewing. "I still embarrassed myself," in interviews, she said. "The 12-week study was far from enough to make a career transformation." She kept going on interviews. "Each time, I got to learn something new and became a little bit stronger.'

By March of 2018, she had been unemployed for almost a year, was running out of money and her visa allowing her to stay in the US was soon to expire. However, she had gained confidence. When she entered the final interview at Airbnb, she had one offer in hand, so was not nervous. It turned out to be a good interview. "They gave me the offer, and all the hard work and sleepless nights paid off," she said.

At the end of her blog post, Kelly listed tips to share, lessons learned and helpful resources. Here is an edited version:

Tips I would love to share

1. Know what you want, set your goal, work really hard to achieve that goal, and never settle for less.

2. Growth mindset, it's really important. Don't say "I'm not good at coding," "I'm not good at stats". It's not about talent. Don't use "talent" to describe others as an excuse for your laziness. What you need is to learn in the right way, and practice many times until you are good.

3. Take note of all the interview questions you got asked, especially those questions you failed to answer. You can fail again, but don't fail at the same spot. You should always be learning and improving.

4. Discuss questions you don't understand with other people if possible. I really appreciate the help from my fellow classmates and instructors at Galvanize, everyone was very supportive and willing to help each other.

5. Go to local data science meetups, join data science learning groups, connect with people in industry, send a personalized note when you are trying to connect with strangers on LinkedIn… Expand your network as much as possible, you don't know which one will open a door for you.

6. Sometimes, the result is a combination of luck and preparation, and you are just not lucky this time. Don't always credit failure to yourself being not good.

What she would do differently if she could restart the job search process

- **Don't interview with the companies that you want to work for at the beginning of your job search, unless**

you think you are ready to go for them.

I started my job search process with an interview with Uber, and I deeply regret that decision. I screwed up so bad that I couldn't get interviews for other teams at Uber. Most people aim at the major tech companies as dream companies; however, most of these companies have a strict rule that if you fail once, you can't take another interview in 6 months or 1 year. Therefore, you want to make sure you are prepared before taking interviews at these companies.

- **Narrow down what types of jobs you want to do, and what types of jobs are not for you, this will save you a lot of time.**

If you have ever looked at the data scientist job postings, you would know how broad the responsibilities can be. There are data scientists who work on natural language processing, computer vision, deep learning, and there are also data scientists who work on A/B tests, product analytics. Making sure what kind of job is a good fit for you and what is not, this will help you save a ton of time in preparing for interviews.

In my case, I skipped all job postings that ask for a Ph.D. degree and knowledge of deep learning, computer vision, etc. But I still have too many areas to learn and prepare. Below is a summary of the resources I used during my job search. Remember, there are too many resources you can use to learn, and you can spend a lot of time just searching for the materials, please be selective and make sure you utilize them to the fullest.

Resources for data science interview preparation

Statistics

- Khan Academy: Very good to learn about basic concepts.
- Practical Statistics for Data Scientists: Good one, very practical, strongly recommend.
- Statistics course by Duke University on Coursera (Taught in R)

Probability questions

- brilliant.org: I purchased their membership when preparing my interviews, and I found it is one of the recommended materials in Facebook's onsite interview prep guide.

A/B test

- Udacity A/B testing course by Google: I watched it twice and wrote a summary of this course.
- KDD papers and slides by Microsoft: A/B test is commonly asked in data

science interviews but not many people outside the industry have ever done an A/B test before, so I searched and read ~15 papers when I was trying to learn about experiment design.

- Slides and videos on Exp Platform
- Company tech blogs, such as Airbnb data science blog

Machine learning

- Stanford University Machine Learning course by Andrew Ng on Coursera
- An Introduction to Statistical Learning: with Applications in R: One of the textbooks we used at Galvanize
- Machine Learning in Action: Another textbook we used at Galvanize
- Applied Data Science with Python Specialization by University of Michigan on Coursera

Basic programming algorithms

- HackerRank: More entry-level friendly
- LeetCode: work on questions from easy or medium level
- Cracking the Coding Interview: 189 Programming Questions and Solutions (Written in Java)

Python data manipulation (Pandas, Numpy)

- Datacamp
- Tip: I improved Python data manipulation tremendously by working on companies' take-home challenges. Practice is the best way to learn.

R

- Sorry I don't use much R. Usually in interviews you can use either R or Python.

SQL

- Mode Analytics SQL Tutorial: I'm fairly familiar with SQL but I still go through this before every SQL interview, especially the advanced section, just in case.

Product sense/Business understanding

- Case in point
- Cracking the PM interview
- Decode and conquer

General interview questions

- Lynda Raynier's Youtube Channel: Really helpful for general interview questions. You can also search for other videos to learn about how to answer a specific interview question.

Other resources

- Company tech blogs: Airbnb, Uber, LinkedIn, Netflix, Lyft, Pinterest, Stitch Fix, Quora, Yelp… You name it. Great resources to learn.
- Collect company's interview questions from Glassdoor before technical interviews.

Parting Thoughts from Kelly

Seeking for a job is just one episode of our life journey. But the grit, passion, and perseverance we carried through the process will benefit us in the long run. Personally, I deeply believe in the quote below and will always continue to believe in it. Hope it motivates you just like how it motivated me:

> "Don't ever let someone tell you that you can't do something. You got a dream, you gotta protect it. People can't do something themselves, they wanna tell you that you can't do it. You want something, go get it. Period."—The Pursuit of Happyness

A Look at AI Education Providers

Udacity Positioning for Public Offering

An outgrowth of free computer science classes offered through Stanford University, Udacity was formally announced in 2012. The company stated in a February 2018 press release that it had revenue of $70 million in 2017, up from $29 million the previous year. It was the first time the company had released any revenue figures. CEO Vishal Makhijani, who replaced founder Sebastian Thrun as CEO two years ago, said the company aspires to one day become a public company.

Udacity started offering online courses in 2014. They last six months on average, in fields including artificial intelligence, self-driving cars and robotics. Makhijano said the revenue growth was fueled by student enrollment, which grew to more than 50,000 last year. Tuition ranges from about $1,000 to $2,400 per course.

Udacity has partnerships with more than 120 companies including Alphabet, Lyft, Uber, Amazon, Mercedes Benz and NVIDIA. Makhijani said the talent pool is not big enough to satisfy the demands from tech companies. "The supply-demand imbalance is out of whack," he said.

Udacity is not yet profitable, and has more than $100 million from investors in the bank. The company has offices in India, China, Germany and the United Arab Emirates. The company has raised $163 million to date and was valued at $1 billion before its last funding round.

When Udacity's Nanodegree Plus program was announced in January 2016, then CEO Thrun also announced a job guarantee for anyone who completed the program within six months of graduation. Udacity recently ended that pledge, stopped accepting new enrollments into the program and ended it in June 2018. The program was priced at $299 per month, $100 more than a regular Nanodegree program.

Asked in an [account in Insider Higher Ed](#) why it was ending the Nanodegree Plus program and its job guarantee, Udacity said in a statement that it was "focused on connecting learning to jobs for all our students." Udacity declined to share data on how many students got their money back or got jobs as a result of the program.

A [report in VentureBeat](#) stated that of some 10,000 students who had earned nanodegrees since 2014, around 1,000 had found jobs as a result, a placement rate of about 10 percent. A Udacity spokesperson said that many Nanodegree participants are already employed and take the course for continuing education. Also, while Nanodegree programs are paid offerings, the company said more than five million students have enrolled in free courses.

Deeplearning.ai from Andrew Ng

Andrew Ng, the founder of Deeplearning.ai, refers to AI as the "new electricity." Ng is a computer scientist who co-founded and led Google Brain, was a former VP and Chief Scientist at Baidu, and is an adjunct professor at Stanford University. He is also an early pioneer of online learning, and a co-founder of Coursera.

In August 2017, Ng announced deeplearning.ai, a sequence of Deep Learning courses offered on Coursera. He stated at the time on the [Coursera blog](), "These courses will help you master Deep Learning, learn how to apply it, and perhaps even find a job in AI."

He added, "Just as electricity transformed every major industry starting about 100 years ago, AI is now poised to do the same. Several large tech companies have already built divisions dedicated to AI, and have made huge strides transforming themselves with AI. But in the next few years, companies of all sizes and across all industries will realize that they too can – and must – be part of this AI-powered future."

He described the course offerings: "Anyone with basic machine learning knowledge can take this sequence of five courses, which make up Coursera's new Deep Learning Specialization. You will learn the basics of neural networks, gain practical skills for building AI systems, learn about backpropagation, convolutional networks, recurrent networks, and more. In hands-on projects, you will practice applying Deep Learning and see it work for yourself on applications in healthcare, computer vision for reading sign language, music generation, language understanding, and others. The

Specialization also includes interviews with some of the top leaders in the field, who will share with you their personal stories and give you advice for your career."

Ng noted that 1.8 million people had enrolled in his Machine Learning class on Coursera since 2011, when it was launched by Ng and four Stanford students.

How Daniel Did It

Here is a mildly edited account from Daniel of Australia, on his experience taking Deep Learning courses via learning.ai. He writes:

The deeplearning.ai specialization is dedicated to teaching you state of the art techniques and how to build them yourself.

If you're a software developer who wants to get into building deep learning models or you've got a little programming experience and want to do the same, this course is for you.

Deep learning and machine learning skills are in demand. If you're after a career change, as I was, this course will set you on the path.

Whatever your reason. Make sure you have one before starting. Write it down It will give you something to refer back to when the learning gets hard. It will be a reminder of why you started.

What are the prerequisites?

The course page lists programming experience and a basic knowledge of mathematics and machine learning as prerequisites.

Python is the language of the choice for the course and much of deep learning. So if you've got at least a few months Python experience or are experienced with other programming languages and ideologies, you should be in a good place.

As for the math, I've never taken a math course outside of high school. If I needed to learn some math for the course, I went to Khan Academy.

Some math topics covered in the course (all linked to Khan Academy).

- Statistics and probability
- Multivariable calculus
- Linear algebra
- Matrices

Before starting the course, I didn't understand all of these in-depth. Andrew Ng, the main lecturer, does a great job explaining enough of the math to get you started during the lectures. For anything deeper, you'll find the links above a great help.

As for machine learning experience, I'd completed Andrew's Machine Learning Course on Coursera prior to starting. Is it 100% required? No. But it did help with a few concepts here and there. The course is free however, it is done in Matlab/Octave which I found a bit more difficult since I had been used to Python.

Overall, if you've got a high school math education and are comfortable to code functions a few lines long in Python, you've got enough to start.

The course is broken into five parts. Each can be done individually but I found them to be great compliments to each other.

Time allocation for each part varies in length between 2–4 weeks and has a recommended study time of 4–5 hours/week. I could usually do a week's worth of classes and assessment in one 6–8 hour day, including breaks. Meaning, the entire course took me about 4–5 weeks.

Part 1: Neural Networks and Deep Learning

This section introduces the concept of neural networks and deep learning. Kind of like the introduction of this post but with actual code and far more depth.

You'll start out by building your own neural networks from scratch and learn a thing or two about Python's numerical library NumPy.

What does from scratch mean?

From scratch is without using any frameworks. Imagine a framework being a collection of code someone else has written to make the code you write smaller (less lines). Some popular deep learning frameworks are Keras, TensorFlow and PyTorch. Whenever you see an article titled, "Best results ever in 11-lines of code," the article probably uses one of these frameworks.

Those same 11-lines of code may turn out to be 50+ in NumPy/pure Python. This first section will run you through the full 50 lines to understand what frameworks are doing behind the scenes.

Part 2: Improving Deep Neural Networks: Hyperparameter tuning, Regularisation and Optimisation

Deep learning is often referred to as a black box, meaning, your model learns things but you're not quite sure how it learns them.

The issue with this is that it can be hard to improve your model when if it isn't working as you'd hoped.

Working through part 2 you'll learn about common deep learning tidbits such as hyperparameter tuning, initialisation, optimisation, mini-batch gradient descent and regularisation.

Woah. Slow down. What's all this jargon?

For now, just think of them as ways to get the most out your neural network.

You'll also get a taste of what it's like to split up your datasets into training, validation and test sets. A training set is where your neural network will learn and validation and testing sets are you can test the robustness of your network on unseen data.

Where part 1 started with Python and NumPy, part 2 will expose you to one of the most popular deep learning libraries, TensorFlow.

Part 3: Structuring Machine Learning Projects

This section is a big one, not in terms of length but in terms of practicality. It's one thing to be able to be able to build machine learning systems but another thing to be able to diagnose them when they go wrong and improve them for future use.

Part 3 takes you through two case studies. You're put in the driver's seat to decide upon how a deep learning system could be used to solve a problem within them. Or how the current deep learning system could be improved.

I've seen teams waste months or years through not understanding the principles taught in this course.— Andrew Ng

Courses two and three are quite unique to the deeplearning.ai specialization. I haven't seen many other courses talk about these topics in the way Andrew does.(Part 4 covers Convolutional Neural Networks and Part 5 covers Sequence Models.)

Extras

For the first half of the specialisation, at the end of each week of classes, there's an interview with a deep learning superhero. Andrew sits down with people such as Yann LeCun and Geoffrey Hinton to discuss the current state of deep learning and where the field is heading. These interviews were one of my favourite parts of the course.

All of the video interviews and lectures are available free on the deeplearning.ai YouTube channel.

Assessment and Course Forums

For access to the course forums and assessment, you'll need to sign up on Coursera.

You've got the details. You know when to start, you know what you're going to learn, now how do you actually do it?

There is no right way to answer this. What worked for me might not work for you.

I used Trello to track my progress. Trello is a free application which helps you visualise your plans. Before starting the course, I mapped out the curriculum onto a board.

How much does it cost?

You can watch all of the course lectures for free on YouTube. But if you sign up for the full Specialisation on Coursera, the cost is $64AUD per month (around $47USD).

The full specialisation is suggested at taking 4–5 months to complete but since I completed it faster, I only paid for 2-months ($128AUD total).

Summary

Out of all the courses I've done, this is by far one of the best. Andrew is a practitioner who weaves his knowledge gained through experience in each of the lessons. He's got skin in the game, so you know what you're being taught has been put into practice.

It was difficult at times. I ran into a bunch of roadblocks. But having the forums and the rest of the internet, I knew I could solve problems as they arrived as long as I was patient.

My two favorite sections were part 3 and part 5. Anything to do with language and communication fascinates me, so part 5 was a real highlight. And it was great to hear Andrew's insider wisdom on how to get the most out of machine learning projects during part 3.

(Andrew is a machine learning engineer at Max Kelson based in Brisbane, Australia, an analytics and software engineering company specializing in machine learning and AI. Write to him at daniel@mrdbourke.com.)

Higher Education Revolution Taking Place?

Three of the 10 most popular courses on Coursera are produced by deeplearning.ai and taught by Andrew Ng. Ng's original MOOC (massive online open course) remains the most popular course offered by Coursera, notes an article in EdSurge published in June 2018. Since the course began in 2012, it has drawn more than 1.7 million enrollments. The new series of AI courses from deeplearning.ai, launched last year, have exceeded 250,000 sign ups. That means hundreds of thousands of students have sat through lecture videos by Ng. As the piece in EdSurge suggested, "In other words, Andrew Ng probably teaches more people than anyone else on the planet, putting him in a position to have an unprecedented impact on an emerging field."

Kian Katanforoosh is the co-creator for the deep learning courses and is listed as the Head Teaching Assistant for all of them. "We think that to shape the future, there is a huge need for AI engineers," he stated in the EdSurge piece. "We're really amazed by the number of people who take the courses."

Now the question stands of whether more education providers will emerge based around a single thinker - Star Scholar U. Would that potentially cut universities out of the picture? Stanford profession Sebastian Thrun founded Udacity, which offers most of its courses outside of colleges and is valued at more than a billion dollars.

The universities offering AI education are not yet running for the hills. Still this new category of learning experience is certainly compelling, for a generation of students cognizant of the potential for student debt to weigh them down as they start of establish financial independence. Maybe there is room for both options, formal education from institutions of higher learning, and online learning from credible experts.

Chapter 5: Salaries, Jobs in AI

Modern time clocks were an objective way to verify how much time workers put on the clock. An AI expert with a PhD could make $300,000 today, or $144 per hour. Contrast that with the federal minimum wage of $7.25 per hour to gain some appreciation of the value of AI expertise in today's market.
Credit: US National Archives.

Salaries in AI High and Getting Higher

Salaries for AI talent are high and getting higher. Demand is great for experienced expertise and the available supply of qualified AI experts is nowhere near enough, creating an opportunity for those who succeed in become qualified.

"Right now, A.I. is an elitist sport – there are very few people who know how to practice it," said Tom

Eck, the CTO of industry platforms at IBM and a software developer who has been involved in AI as far back as the early '90s. "The top-tier AI researchers are getting paid the salaries of NFL quarterbacks, which tells you the demand and the perceived value." Eck was speaking at an event in New York reported by Dice.

The Dice Salary Calculator suggests that a tech pro in San Francisco with at least five years' experience in technologies related to artificial intelligence (including data analytics and natural-language processing) can earn as much as $121,000 per year; in a "cooler" market like Kansas City, salaries can still approach (and often exceed) six figures. Maybe that's not what an NFL quarterback makes, but that's still really good. (See Dice salary scale.)

A tax filing by research lab OpenAI made public by a piece in the New York TImes in April 2018, shed more light on the magnitude of salaries for top AI talent. OpenAI paid its top research, Ilya Sutskever (see photo) more than $1.9 million in 2016. It paid another researcher, Ian Goodfellow, more than $800,000. Both were recruited from Google. A third name in the field, roboticist Pieter Abbeel, made $425,000, after taking a leave being a professor at the University of California, Berkeley. The figures include signing bonuses.

OpenAI is a non profit, thus cannot offer stock options. So some have suggested these researchers may have undersold themselves.

Founded in 2015 by Elon Musk of Tesla and other well-known figures in the tech industry, OpenAI appeals to idealists by promising not to create technology that could be a danger to people. "I turned down offers for multiple times the dollar amount I accepted at OpenAI," Mr. Sutskever said. "Others did the same."

OpenAI spent about $11 million in its first year, with more than $7 million going to salaries and other employee benefits. It employed 52 people in 2016.

People who work at major tech companies or have entertained job offers from them told The New York Times that AI specialists with little or no industry experience can make between $300,000 and $500,000 a year in salary and stock. Top names can receive compensation packages that extend into the millions.

"The amount of money was borderline crazy," Wojciech Zaremba, a researcher who joined OpenAI after internships at Google and Facebook, told Wired. While he would not reveal exact numbers, Mr. Zaremba said big tech companies were offering him two or three times what he believed his real market value was.

At DeepMind, a London AI lab now owned by Google, costs for 400 employees totaled $138 million in 2016, according to the company's annual financial filings in Britain. That translates to

$345,000 per employee, including researchers and other staff.

Researchers like Mr. Sutskever specialize in what are called neural networks, complex algorithms that learn tasks by analyzing vast amounts of data. They are used in everything from digital assistants in smartphones to self-driving cars.

Some researchers may command higher pay because their names carry weight across the AI community and they can help recruit other researchers.

Mr. Sutskever was part of a three-researcher team at the University of Toronto that worked on computer vision technology. Mr. Goodfellow invented a technique that allows machines to create fake digital photos that are nearly indistinguishable from the real thing.

Sizing the AI Talent Pool

Element AI, an independent lab in Canada, estimates that 22,000 people worldwide have the skills needed to do serious AI research — about double from a year ago. "There is a mountain of demand and a trickle of supply," said Chris Nicholson, the chief executive and founder of Skymind, a start-up working on AI, to the New York Times.

"When you hire a star, you are not just hiring a star," Mr. Nicholson of the start-up Skymind said.

"You are hiring everyone they attract. And you are paying for all the publicity they will attract."

Though the pool of available A.I. researchers is growing, it is not growing fast enough. "If anything, demand for that talent is growing faster than the supply of new researchers, because AI is moving from early adopters to wider use," Mr. Nicholson said.

Pricey hires might be necessary, suggested Kai-Fu Lee, who previously ran Google's business in China, told an audience of CEOs at this year's World Economic Forum in Davos, Switzerland. "Google is paying a million dollars for these superstars," said Lee, now a venture capitalist, quoted in an account in Bloomberg Businessweek. "You may not need someone that high, but you've got to break the scale for at least one person."

The supply of AI experts is not a universally accepted figure. The Element AI report said of the 22,000 Ph.D.-level computer scientists skilled in AI, about 3,000 were currently looking for a job. But the US alone had 10,000 available positions, according to Element CEO Jean-Francois Gagne, quoted in Bloomberg.

Tencent Holdings of China estimated in December 2017 that the world had 200,000 to 300,000 "AI practitioners and researchers." Element said Tencent counted too many coders who contribute to projects but lack the expertise to create novel algorithms and applications from scratch.

Bloomberg suggested that AI services companies such as Element have an "incentive to highlight scarcity." In response, Gagne stated, "The talent shortage is real," and that his company has also been challenged to hire the qualified people it needs. At the current education rate, an influx of new experts will start to moderate salaries in three to four years, he suggested.

Salaries by AI Title from Indeed

At present, demand for AI talent is exploding. The job search site Indeed reported in August that between June 2015 and June 2018, the number of job postings with "AI" or "machine learning" increased by nearly 100%. The percent of searches for these terms on Indeed also increased by 182%, the Indeed report found, as reported in TechRepublic.

"There is a growing need by employers for AI talent," Raj Mukherjee, senior vice president of product at Indeed, told TechRepublic. "As companies continue to adopt solutions or develop their own in-house it is likely that demand by employers for these skills will continue to rise."

Some 94% of job postings that contained AI or machine learning terminology were for machine learning engineers, the report found. And 41% of machine learning engineer positions were still open after 60 days.

Other job titles in high demand included data scientists (found in 75% of AI job postings), computer vision engineers (65%), and algorithm engineers (37%).

Here are the 10 highest-paying AI jobs, and their average salary in the US, according to Indeed.

1. Director of analytics

Average salary: $140,837

2. Principal scientist

Average salary: $138,271

3. Machine learning engineer

Average salary: $134,449

4. Computer vision engineer

Average salary: $134,346

5. Data scientist

Average salary: $130,503

6. Data engineer

Average salary: $125,999

7. Algorithm engineer

Average salary: $104,112

8. Computer scientist

Average salary: $97,850

9. Statistician

Average salary: $83,731

10. Research engineer

Average salary: $71,600

The report also examined the cities with the highest concentration of AI jobs. New York came in at no. 1, with nearly 12% of all AI job postings concentrated there, followed by San Francisco (10%) and San Jose (9%). Washington, DC (8%) and Boston (6%) rounded out the top five.

View from Paysa

The career advisory service company Paysa did an analysis in late 2017 of 142 profiles in its system, finding that an AI engineer earns an average of $171,715, ranging from $124,542 at the 25th percentile to $201,853 at the 75th percentile. The top earners (the top 10%) earned more than $257,530. Compensation includes base salary, equity and bonus.

In technical skills, career advisory service Paysa found 54% of the sample knew Java, 44% knew C++ and 36% knew Python. Most had up to two years of experience on the job.

Companies paying the most for AI engineers Paysa found were: Uber, at $314,746; WalmartLabs, at $265,698; Netflix at $264,799; Facebook at $257,799; Salesforce at $248,281; and Google at $236,388.

The top metro areas for AI jobs and the average salary employees can expect to receive were: 1. San Francisco, at $182,418; 2. Seattle at $191,213; New York at $122,075; Boston at $151,806; and Chicago at $102,768.

"AI investment is exploding now, more than ever, at a rapid pace across every industry," said Chris Bolte, co-founder and CEO of Paysa. "Between the need to leverage massive amounts of data and deliver the highly personalized experiences that today's connected consumer requires, new career and salary opportunities for AI talent are popping up every day and seem to be never ending. This is great news for today's workers on many levels and squelches the fear that AI will eliminate the need for humans in the workplace."

Note to the AI ambitious: Catch the wave while you can because if Element CEO Jean-Francois Gagne is right, AI salaries will moderate in three to four years.

Chapter 6: AI and Ethics

Eleanor Roosevelt and the Universal Declaration of Human Rights in 1958. In a related speech, she said: "Where, after all, do universal human rights begin? In small places, close to home—so close and so small that they cannot be seen on any maps of the world. Yet they are the world of the individual person; the neighborhood he lives in; the school or college he attends; the factory, farm, or office where he works." Some are suggesting the same perspective is needed on AI and ethics today.
Credit: US National Archives

Power and Potential of AI Raises Ethics Awareness

AI is powerful and has the potential to do tremendous good. At the same time, we are exposed to the risk that powerful AI can exhibit bias, such as through unexplained algorithms, or data sets that skew results in an unfair way. It might not matter so much for shopping experiences, but when the AI system is advising on freedom or incarceration, or what gets sacrificed by an AI self-driving car, then the implications are serious.

That context is giving rise to an increased focus and urgency on the ethics around AI. An editorial in Science published in August suggested international cooperation will be needed to harness the power of AI for good.

"From diagnosing cancer and understanding climate change to delivering risky and consuming jobs, AI is already showing its potential for good," said Mariarosaria Taddeo, deputy director of the Digital Ethics Lab at Oxford University, one of the authors of the commentary, interviewed by Wired. "The question is how can harness this potential?"

The potential for AI to do good is immense, said Taddeo. Technology using AI will have the capability to tackle issues "from environmental disasters to financial crises, from crime, terrorism and war, to famine, poverty, ignorance, inequality, and appalling living standards," she says.

For example, AI has already been used to sift through hundreds of bird sounds to estimate when songbirds arrived at their Arctic breeding grounds. This kind of analysis will allow researchers to understand how migratory animals are responding to climate change. Another way we are learning about climate change is through images of coral. An AI trained by looking at hundreds of pictures of coral helped researchers to discover a new species this year, and the technique will be used to analyse coral's resistance to ocean warming.

The risk in the power of AI is exemplified in self-driving cars that get involved in fatal accidents.

Determining who is responsible is a work in progress. The potential for AI systems to unfairly discriminate, with serious consequences, is exemplified by the use of Compas, the risk assessment tool developed by Northpointe, Inc., and used by the Wisconsin Department of Corrections to advise on parole cases. The system was found to discriminate against African-American and Hispanic men. A team of journalists researched 10,000 criminal defendants in Broward County, Fla., and found the system predicted black defendants posed a higher rate of recidivism than they actually do in reality, and the system predicted the opposite result for white defendants.

GDPR's Article 22 Sharpens Focus on Privacy

Big data feeds AI systems. More data is needed to make the systems more accurate in their ability to predict. The big players such as Facebook, Google and Amazon, need to collect, store and manipulate as much data as possible, to keep their business models going. The idea that users need to grant permission for their data to be collected and manipulated, and that users need to understand what they are allowing when they become users the implications of these and other sites, is gaining steam.

This privacy push is examplied in Article 22 of the European General Data Protection Regulation (GDPR), which took effect in May 2018.

Article 22(1) states that *"The data subject shall have the right not to be subject to a decision based solely on automated processing, including profiling, which produces legal effects concerning him or her or similarly significantly affects him or her"*. In its draft guidelines, the WP categorically states that, as a rule, under Article 22 there is a prohibition on fully automated individual decision-making, including profiling that has a legal or similarly significant effect.

Lots of interpretation is going on about the implications of Article 22. An account in [Hogan Lovells Chronicle of Data Protection](#) says, "What this interpretation means in practice is that if the data processing behind online advertising activities strays into the realm of making decisions that significantly affect individuals, this processing is, by default, prohibited. It will then be for those involved in online advertising activities to obtain explicit consent (note the higher standard of what is already a very tough standard!) in order to lawfully use the data."

A number of initiatives have come about to pursue ethics in AI. These include AI4People, the first global forum in Europe on the social impact of AI. Participants in the EU Declaration on Cooperation on AI, signed early in 2018, pledged to work together on AI ethics and using AI for good purposes.

The Partnership on AI to Benefit People and Society, which the authors of the Science editorial are members of, was founded in late 2016. "We designed the Partnership on AI, in part, so that we can invest more attention and effort on harnessing AI to contribute to solutions for some of humanity's most challenging problems, including making advances in health and wellbeing, transportation, education, and the sciences" said Eric Horvitz and

Mustafa Suleyman, the Partnership on AI's founding co-chairs, in the interview for Wired.

"The debate on the governance of AI needs to involve scientists, academics, engineers, lawyers, policy-makers, politicians, civil society and business representatives" said Taddeo in Wired. "We need to understand the nature of post-AI societies and the values that should underpin the design, regulation, and use of AI in these societies."

"In this respect, AI is not different from electricity or steam engines" says Taddeo. "It is our responsibility to steer the use of AI in such a way to foster human flourishing and well-being and mitigate the risks that this technology brings about."

The Science editorial emphasises the need for users to protect their "self-determination." Here is an excerpt: "As AI becomes invisibly ubiquitous, new ethical challenges emerge. The protection of human self-determination is one of the most relevant and must be addressed urgently. The application of AI to profile users for targeted advertising, as in the case of online service providers, and in political campaigns, as unveiled by the Cambridge Analytica case, offer clear examples of the potential of AI to capture users' preferences and characteristics and hence shape their goals and nudge their behavior to an extent that may undermine their self-determination."

Techniques to explain how AI makes its decisions and recommendations, will be important to pursue.

The Explainable AI program of the Defense Advanced Research Project Agency (DARPA) is one example. The goal of the program is to define new techniques to explain the decision-making process of AI systems, to enable users to understand how the systems work, and designers and developer to improve the systems to mitigate the risk of misuse. The Science editorial suggested an "ethical impact analysis" is needed in the beginning of major AI projects, to assess benefits and risks, and define guiding principles for ethically sound design.

Forum at Harvard University Points to Urgency of AI and Ethics Discussion

Many of these same themes were sounded at a recent gathering of an elite group of academics, scientists, researchers and standard-setters came at Harvard University in September to bring new urgency to a discussion of AI and ethics.

The speakers, brought together as a meeting of the AI World Society Initiative under the auspices of the Michael Dukakis Institute for Leadership and Innovation, suggested in this area of exponential advances in AI, the time is now for the discussion. The event was covered by AI Trends.

"We would like to ensure that AI and robotics will be used for the good of humanity. The greatest danger I see is from unconstrained machine learning, where the system can define goals not intended by the designer." said Matthias Scheutz, director of the Human-Robot Interaction Lab at Tufts University. "The challenge for us now is to have the larger discussion."

Dr. Scheutz, who has a Phd. in philosophy from the University of Vienna and a joint Phd. in Cognitive Science and Computer Science from Indiana University, is working on a way to safeguard AI algorithms in chip design.

"The best way to safeguard AI systems is to build ethical mechanisms into the algorithms themselves," he said. "We need to do ethical testing of the system without the system knowing it. That requires specialized hardware and a virtual machine architecture."

He showed a slide depicting a copy of a system being subject to an ethical test; if it fails, the primary system can be terminated. "Special hardware chips have to be legally mandated of the hardware companies, so that all the microprocessors have the tools built in," he said. More research is needed to flesh out the proposal, which he intends to bring forward.

The speakers were realistic about the difficulty of the challenge. "Usually AI scientists don't have ethics as a priority," said Nazli Choucri, a professor of political science at MIT. "It's not part of the job description." The author of 11 books and many articles, Dr. Choucri is a member of the European Academy of Sciences.

Marc Rotenberg, president of the Electronic Privacy Information Center (EPIC) takes the position that, "Knowledge of AI algorithms is a fundamental right." EPIC has filed a number of suits in pursuit of disclosure, including one to compel the TSA to share information on how they create profiles for air travelers.

The mission includes bringing the message to Washington, D.C. "We're trying to get the administration to create a public process, an open debate on US AI policy," said Rotenberg, who teaches information privacy and open government at Georgetown Law and frequently testifies before Congress on emerging privacy and civil liberties issues. "We want there to be a mechanism for public participation. We think algorithmic transparency will be a key in policy formulation."

The international Organization for Economic Cooperation and Development (OECD), founded in 1961 and now with 36 countries as members, has been working on AI guidelines. He noted that, "The Japanese have put forward a set of simple principles that can be easily understood," that emphasize collaboration and acknowledge risk. "There is urgency to this issue. The gap between informed government decision-making and the reality of progress is growing," Rotenberg said.

China is a non-member of the OECD but has a working relationship. Rotenberg noted that China is engaged in an extensive data collection effort on its citizens. "Here is a warning to the Chinese," he said, "There is great risk to all governments that they will lose control of these systems."

Competition Between Countries

How AI will is affecting the competition between countries is coming into focus. "We have a lot of attention on the US-China competition in AI," said Joseph Nye, professor at Harvard University and former dean of the John F. Kennedy School of Government at Harvard. "China wants to surpass the US in AI and Eric Schmidt [former executive chairman of Google and its parent, Alphabet], believes it could happen by 2030. That has gotten the attention of the US Congress."

Nye described an "AI arms race" for geopolitical leadership, a competition between states to have their military forces equipped with the best AI. Some suggest the AI arms race has already begun. "That leads to policy discussions, such as on to what extent we want Chinese students at MIT and Caltech? We have always had a free and liberal university system. But if a student goes home and helps China get a leg up, should that be allowed?"

He noted that Congress is preventing China from buying certain US startups. "Should we restrict access to students if they would compete with us on AI?" he asked.

While he said he personally would not favor such restrictions, the international competition could have "profound effects" on the free and open university system of the US.

Equating the advance of AI with the availability of nuclear weapons, Nye stepped through decades of international efforts to restrict the use of nuclear weapons since 1945: a proposed UN Nuclear Test Ban Treaty in 1954; an accepted Partial Test Ban Treaty in 1963; a Non-Proliferation Treaty on Nuclear Weapons in 1968, and the Strategic Arms Limitation Agreement between the US and Soviet Union in 1972.

"It takes a long time and the first efforts don't go to the heart of the problem," he said. Still, nations do agree to restrain themselves when it's in their self-interest. "Previous experience has shown us that norms can work, but it takes time, decades," Nye said. "Do we have decades for AI? Can we speed it up? Is this a Sputnik moment?," he queried, referring to the first satellite launched into space by the Soviet Union in 1957, beating the US and leading to an intense effort to catch up.

All agreed on the importance of having "humans in the loop," to require human interactions that can restrain autonomous AI systems when necessary. "The key is to make sure that humans remain in command," Nye said. "We're in the early stage of something that will take a good deal of time. The question is, do we have that time?"

The US and China differ in their systems of government and in attitudes towards human rights, for example, privacy. China is known to have embarked on a system to document it citizens using facial recognition, what Nye referred to as a system of "mass surveillance."

This idea was reinforced by Dr. Hyunjin Seo, an associated professor in the School of Journalism at the University of Kansas, and a Harvard University fellow, who had recently travelled to China. She observed, "The Chinese government is putting in place more extensive control over their citizens," especially through the use of cameras.

Military Putting Emphasis on Ethics

The US military is putting a high priority on teaching ethics these days. "Every person in the military today is trained on a way to question the ethics of an order," said Tom Creely, a professor at the US Naval War College. He teaches a course called Ethics of technology, which now has 17 students who study AI, biotechnology, nanotechnology, information technology - "anything that can be weaponized." he said, adding "Ethics is essential to what we are doing. It's an important topic in the military. And national security is no longer just the Defense Department's problem. We all need to be part of the conversation."

Different Perspective on "AI Arms Race"

A different perspective on the interaction of China and the US about AI is expressed in a provocative new book by Kai-Fu Lee, chairman of Sinovation

Ventures and the past founding president of Google China. He spoke about his new book, "AI Superpowers: China, Silicon Valley and the New World Order," recently in the Washington Post. Here is an excerpt:

"An AI arms race would be a grave mistake. The AI boom is more akin to the spread of electricity in the early Industrial Revolution than nuclear weapons during the Cold War. Those who take the arms-race view are more interested in political posturing than the flourishing of humanity. The value of AI as an omni-use technology rests in its creative, not destructive, potential."

Chapter 7: AI Self-Driving Cars

Forensic Analysis of Tesla Crash Based on Preliminary NTSB June 2018 Report

By Lance Eliot, the AI Trends Insider

Based on the June 7, 2018 release of the preliminary NTSB report about the fatal car crash of a Tesla on March 23, 2018, I provide in today's column an initial forensic analysis of the incident.

Keep in mind that the just released NTSB report (about three days ago as of the writing of this column) is very slim on details at this juncture of the investigation and so there really isn't much in terms of facts and evidence that would allow for a thorough analysis. Nonetheless, it is instructive to be able to try and piece together the clues released to-date and see if useful insights can be gleaned.

Learning From the "Past"

At the Cybernetic AI Self-Driving Car Institute, we are developing AI systems for self-driving cars. As a result, we are keenly interested in what happens in incidents involving self-driving cars, along with wanting to provide insights for auto makers and other tech firms that are in the midst of developing and maintaining such AI systems.

As per the famous quote of philosopher George Santayana: "Those who cannot remember the past are condemned to repeat it." With the rapid advances taking place with AI self-driving cars, and with the use of our public roadways as part of a grand experiment to see whether self-driving cars are viable, it is especially crucial that we all look at every morsel of what is taking place and try to as rapidly as possible consider what action is most appropriate to ensure the safety of us all.

For some of you, you might say that the risks of any self-driving car endangerment are simply the presumed calculated risk of the person that has opted to drive such a car. This though is narrow thinking and does not include the proper larger scope. The human driver is certainly taking a risk, but so too would any occupants in the car that are accompanying the car with the human driver – suppose the driver has children in the car, are those children able to also calculate the risks involved?

I mention this because at some of my presentations around the country there are at times self-driving car pundits that stand-up and say that it should be each person's own choice as to whether or not they want to drive a self-driving car, and that the government and anyone else should stay out of it. If the driver of a self-driving car was able to drive the car in a manner that was completely isolated from all of the rest of us, I likely would agree that it could be an informed personal decision to make.

We must though keep in mind that driving on our public roadways is a societal interaction and therefore would seemingly be a societal decision. It is for this reason that driving by humans is deemed a "privilege" and not a "right" per se. The Department of Motor Vehicles (DMV) in most states lays out what a human driver must do and not do, in order to retain the privilege to drive a car on our public roadways. There isn't an irrevocable right to drive on our public roadways. It's a revocable privilege.

Context of the Tesla Incident

Here's some key aspects about the Tesla incident, based on using the NTSB preliminary report. On a relatively sunny and dry day in California on Friday, March 23, 2018, in the morning around 9:30 a.m.

PDT a Tesla Model X P100D 2017 was being driven southbound on the multi-lane US Highway 101 (US-101) in Mountain View and was nearing the interchange with the State Highway 85 (SH-85).

Notice that I've mentioned some important aspects already. Was the incident occurring on a rainy day? No. It was sunny and the roads were dry. This is important because we might otherwise need to consider the weather as a factor in what occurred. I think it is relatively sound to assume that weather was not a factor since the roads were dry and it was sunny. Was it nighttime or daytime when the incident occurred? It was daytime, and nearing mid-morning, and so it would have been relatively well lit. I mention this because if it were say nighttime, we'd need to consider the impact of darkness and how it could have diminished the capability of the cameras used for the self-driving car.

You might wonder why I am laboring to mention these nuances. I hope that you'll see the "magic" behind doing a forensic analysis. It is crucial to consider each piece of evidence and try to use it for putting together the puzzle.

The Tesla at the time of the incident was in the High Occupancy Vehicle (HOV) lane, which was the second lane from the left of the median that divides the southbound and northbound lanes. Normally it is permitted to travel in the HOV lane when you have multiple occupants, while in this case there was a solo driver, but since the Tesla is an electric car it qualifies to go in the HOV. The human driver was a 38-year-old male and sadly he died as a result of the crash.

The NTSB indicates they have examined "performance data downloaded from the vehicle." What we don't yet know is what this actually means. Did the Tesla have an Event Data Recorder (EDR)? This EDR is a so-called black box that is akin to the black box that are used in airplanes and helpful when determining why an airplane crashed. Or, did the NTSB have to get various memory dumps from other processors in the Tesla, and if so, which ones and what ones weren't available perhaps due to being destroyed or damaged? Has the NTSB gotten access to data that would have been transmitted potentially to the Tesla cloud that allows for OTA (Over The Air) updates? We don't yet know the depth and extent of the data that the NTSB has collected or intends to collect.

The Crash Itself

The NTSB report indicates that the Tesla was going at about 71 miles per hour when it struck the tail-end of a concrete median that had a "crash attenuator" as an additional barrier at its leading edge. You've probably seen these attenuators before and yet didn't know they had a name. It is a special kind of barrier that is setup to help try and "soften" the blow of a car that crashes into the finger-point of a concrete median. Years ago, traffic studies showed that when cars hit directly a concrete median at the edge point, it pretty much is like slicing bread with a knife. Thus, the thought was to put something at the edge that would dampen the blow. In some cases, you'll see those bright yellow barrels that are filled with sand or sometimes water.

What's an interesting added twist is that the NTSB report says that the attenuator had been previously damaged. It would be helpful if the NTSB could say more about this. Was the attenuator so damaged that it could no longer perform as intended?

I mention this aspect since by-and-large humans are generally able to visually figure out when they see an attenuator that is indeed an attenuator, and humans have the "common sense" that it is there to safe lives and that if you are driving toward it you are likely making a big mistake because it is there when behind it is something fierce like a concrete median. Did the camera of the Tesla capture images of the attenuator? Did the AI system examine the images and detect that within the image was an attenuator? We don't yet know, since the NTSB report doesn't say anything about this.

It is possible that the Tesla AI system has used machine learning to try and determine what attenuators look like. This can be done via the use of artificial neural networks that are trained on thousands and thousands of images of attenuators. Generally, one would like to assume that the Tesla AI has been trained sufficiently to recognize an attenuator, but suppose that this one was damaged in such a way that it no longer well-matched the training images? It is conceivable that the AI system did not thusly categorize the attenuator as an attenuator, and might have classified it as some unknown object, if it detected it at all.

The NTSB report does not indicate what kind of sensors were used on this particular Tesla Model X. It would be crucial for the NTSB to indicate what sensors were used, and also whether it was known as to whether or not the sensors were in working order at the time leading up to the crash. We don't yet know.

I am going to guess that it might have had these sensors (please don't hold me to this, it is just an educated guess based on what normally would be included):

- Rearward Looking Side Cameras: 100 meters (about 328 feet)
- Wide Forward Camera: 60 meters (about 197 feet)
- Main Forward Camera: 150 meters (about 492 feet)
- Narrow Forward Camera: 250 meters (about 820 feet)
- Rear View Camera: 50 meters (about 164 feet)
- Ultrasonic: 8 meters (about 26 feet)
- Forward Looking Side Camera: 80 meters (about 262 feet)
- Radar: 160 meters (about 524 feet)

I've also indicated the typical ranges of the considered maximum detection for each of those devices. This is important to know since the analysis of a crash involves determining how many feet or meters away could the AI system have potentially detected something. In the case of the Uber incident in Arizona, I had used the reported speed of the car to then try to ascertain how far in-advance of the crash could the AI have potentially detected the object in the roadway (it was a pedestrian walking a bicycle). Knowing the type of sensors and their detection ranges is vital to such an analysis.

The Counterclockwise Spin

Per the NTSB report for the Mountain View incident, the report says that the Tesla struck the attenuator while going 71 mile per hour, and then the impact "rotated the Tesla counterclockwise" and ultimately "caused a separation of the front portion of the vehicle." I think we can all agree that hitting something like the attenuator at a speed of 71 miles per hour is going to exert a tremendous amount of force and it certainly seems to have been the case since it caused the front of the Tesla to become separated. It was a hard hit. I don't think anyone can dispute that.

What's interesting is the notion that the Tesla spun counterclockwise. I've not yet seen anyone comment about this aspect. I'll speculate about it. If the Tesla had hit the attenuator fully head-on, we would need to study the physics of the result, but it generally might not have lead to a spin of the Tesla. More than likely, the Tesla probably hit at a front-edge of the car, such as toward the left side of the front edge or to the right of the front edge. This would be more likely to generate a spinning action after the impact. Since the Tesla apparently spun counterclockwise, we'll assume for the moment that it hit at the left side edge of the front of the Tesla, which then jammed the left side against the attenuator, and the right side of the Tesla continued forward which caused it to pivot from the leftside, making it go counterclockwise. This is all speculation and we'll need to see what the NTSB has to say about it.

I'll explain in a moment why I think this counterclockwise spinning is a useful clue.

Aftermath of the Crash

After having crashed and spun, the Tesla was involved in subsequent collisions involving two other cars that were presumably driving southbound and got inadvertently caught up in the incident. I'll assume for now that those additional crashes had nothing to do with the initial crash per se, and were just part of the aftermath.

I am saddened that those subsequent crashes occurred, and it also serves as a reminder about my earlier remarks that incidents involving self-driving cars aren't necessarily confined to impacting just the driver but can also include other innocents that get caught up in the cascading impacts. According to the NTSB report, one of those other drivers suffered minor injuries, and the other was uninjured. I'd say that's nearly a miracle. No matter what led to the initial crash, any aftermath can often be horrific.

The NTSB report further mentions that the 400-volt lithium-ion high-voltage battery in the Tesla caught fire as it was breached during the incident, and a post-crash fire ensued (these can be intense fires; the fire department arrived and was able to put out the fire).

Layout of the Crash Scene

The NTSB preliminary report does not depict a layout of the crash scene. I've used Google Maps to try and see if I can figure out what the crash scene was like.

Based on what I can discern, it appears that the crash occurred at the split of the US-101 continuing forward and an exit ramp to get onto the SH-85 as a left-side offshoot. There appears to be a triangular shaped "gore area" that divides the two. I'm sure you've seen this kind of thing before. You have two lanes that are running next to each other, and at some point up ahead they split from each other. At that splitting or fork, one lane goes straight ahead, while the other veers off. In-between the split is a triangular area that divides the two splitting lanes. In this case, there was a concrete median in that gore area and it had the attenuator at the front-edge of the concrete median.

It appears that there was for a while two HOV lanes leading up to the split. One HOV lane was for those continuing on US-101, and the other was for those cars wanting to veer off to the left as part of the exit from the US-101 leading to the SH-85.

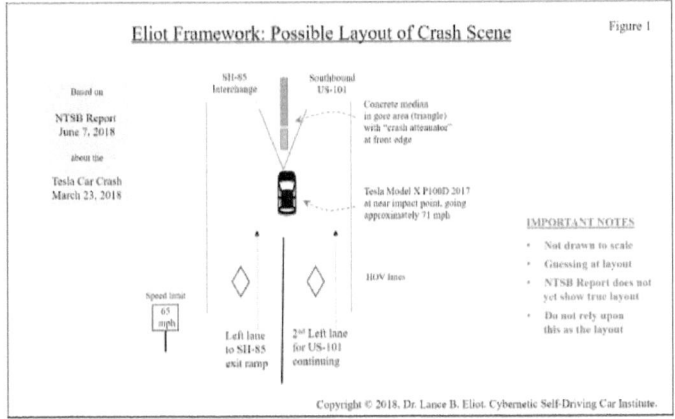

Timing of the Crash

The vital aspects about the crash are contained in the timing aspects reported so far by the NTSB.

According to the NTSB, at 18 minutes 55 seconds before the crash, the Autopilot was engaged. It apparently remained engaged the entire time thereafter. This is important because if the Autopilot was not engaged then we likely wouldn't be discussing any of this, it would generally have been a traditional crash since the Tesla would have been operating like any everyday car. Also, if the Autopilot had suddenly been engaged just seconds before the crash, we might be of a mind to say that the Autopilot had insufficient time to get started and so it was not especially a participant in the crash. In this case, it seems like the Autopilot had been on, it had been on for quite some time before the crash, and it was still on at the time of the crash.

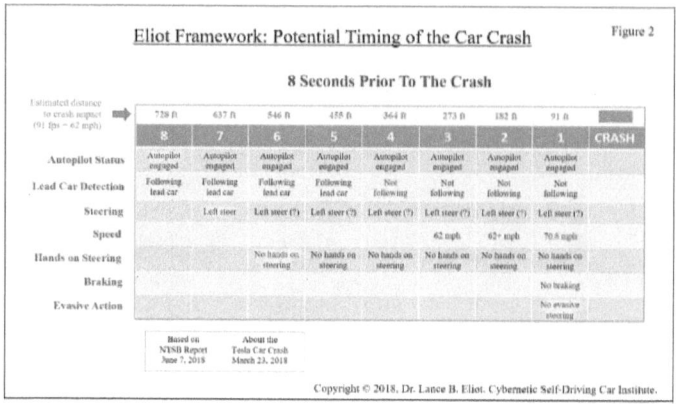

The Tesla was reportedly following a lead car, doing so at 8 seconds before the crash (and might have been doing so even longer, but we don't yet know), and at 4 seconds before the crash it was no longer following a lead car. For those of you not familiar with self-driving cars, they often use a pied piper approach to driving. They spot a car ahead, and then try to match to the pace of that car. If the car ahead speeds-up, the self-driving car will speed-up, but only to some maximum such as the speed limit or perhaps what has been set on the cruise control via the human driver in the self-driving car. If the car ahead slows down, the self-driving car tends to slow down.

As I've said many times before, this pied piper approach is extremely simplistic. It's what a teenage novice driver does when they are first learning to drive, but they quickly realize there are many downsides to this approach. If the approach is not augmented by more sophisticated driving techniques, it's something that has only limited utility. By the way, keep in mind that the Tesla models of today are considered at a Level 2 or Level 3, but are not yet at a true Level 5, which is a self-driving car for which the AI can entirely drive the car without any human intervention. At the levels less than 5, the human driver is considered the driver of the car, in spite of whatever else the "self-driving car" can do or is suggested or implied that it can do.

Once the lead car was no longer ahead of the Tesla, the Tesla then reportedly increased speed, since it was going at 62 miles per hour while following the lead car, and then with a presumed clear space ahead it opted to increase speed to 71 miles per hour at the time of the crash. This "makes sense" in that the system will aim to go to the maximum allowed speed if it believes that there is no car ahead of it that would impede doing so. The NTSB says that the driver had set the cruise control to a maximum of 75 miles per hour, and so the Tesla was likely trying to accelerate to that stated speed. As a side note, the NTSB points out that the speed limit in that location is only 65 miles per hour.

What's especially intriguing in the NTSB preliminary report is that supposedly the Tesla was left steering, doing so at 7 seconds before the crash. The implication is that this continued until the actual crash. What was causing the Tesla to left steer? We aren't sure that it was the human driver, since the NTSB says that there weren't any hands on the steering wheel at 6 seconds to go, and nor until the crash. We also don't know how much left steering was involved – was it a radical left or just a mild torque to the left?

Per the NTSB, there was no pre-crash braking by the Tesla. This implies that neither the human driver hit the brakes, and nor did the Autopilot system. Per the NTSB, there was no evasive steering. This implies that neither the human driver tried to steer clear of the crash, and nor did the Autopilot system.

This then is the conundrum.

We have a car going about 70 miles per hour that plowed into the gore area and unabatedly slammed into the attenuator that was at the end of the concrete median and did so without any apparent indication by the behavior of the car that it was about to happen.

The human driver did not try to stop the car. The human driver did not try to avoid the attenuator by swerving the car. Any of these options were presumably available in that we can assume reasonably that the brakes were operational and that the steering wheel was operational, as far as we know.

The Autopilot system did not try to stop the car. The Autopilot system did not try to avoid the attenuator by swerving the car. Any of these options were presumably available in that we can assume reasonably that the brakes were operational and that the steering was operational and that the Autopilot system had an ability to command those controls, as far as we know.

Before I launch into speculation about how this occurred, let's add some other elements to the situation. The speed of 62 miles per hour is about the same as going 91 feet per second. The speed of 71 miles per hour is about the same as going 104 feet per second. The usual rule-of-thumb for proper driving practices is to maintain a distance of about 1 car length for every 10 miles per hour of speed. Most human drivers don't do this, and they often are very unsafe in terms of the distance they maintain from a car ahead of them. In any case, most self-driving car systems try to maintain the proper recommended distance.

The Tesla Model X is approximately 16 feet in length. So, going at about 60 miles per hour, it presumably was trying to maintain a distance of about (60 mph / 10) x 16 = 96 feet, or 6 car lengths. In the timeline, this would mean that the Tesla was about one second behind the lead car.

Where did the lead car go? Did it opt to get out of the HOV lane and maybe went into the lane to the right? In which case, this implies that in one second of time, from 5 seconds out to the 4 seconds out, it changed lanes and got into the next lane over. Or, did it maybe switch into the exit ramp lane to the left? We don't know.

Or, did the Tesla move to the left from the 7 seconds out to the 4 seconds out, using up 3 seconds, moving so much so that it was no longer directly in the HOV lane that it had been using to follow the lead car? Thus, the lead car never made any lane change, and it was instead the Tesla that essentially did so, and therefore it no longer detected the lead car that was in the prior HOV lane that the Tesla had been presumably squarely in.

It could be that the Tesla was shifting to the left and ended-up not yet being fully in the exit ramp lane, and nor any longer fully in the ongoing HOV lane. It was in-between. Suppose it had not yet fully ended-up in the exit ramp to the left, and then struck the attenuator at the left side of the front of the Tesla. This fits with the aspect earlier that the Tesla then did a counterclockwise spin (I told you that I'd bring this back into the analysis).

In this case, one scenario is that the Tesla was following a lead car, and for which this seemed perfectly normal and common, and then with just a few seconds before impact with the attenuator, and for reasons yet unknown, the Tesla began to shift to the left, as though it was going to get out of the existing HOV lane and into the exit ramp lane but did so without sufficient urgency.

Did the Autopilot intend to actively switch lanes? Or, did it somehow lose itself in terms of the markings on the roadway and it was unsure of where the lane really was?

Why didn't the human driver take over the controls and do something? One explanation is that with only about 3 seconds left to go, which is the point at which the Tesla was apparently no longer following the lead car, the human driver might not have had sufficient time to realize what was happening. Up until then, perhaps the human driver was watching the car ahead and assumed that as long as the car ahead was ahead, it was safe to continue allowing the Autopilot to drive the car.

Was the human driver paying attention to the road? Maybe yes, maybe no – we don't know. The NTSB says that for the 60 seconds before the crash, the human driver put their hands on the steering wheel on 3 occasions for a total of 34 seconds. This implies that within that last minute, the human driver possibly was paying attention to the driving task.

The Tesla has a steering wheel touch indicator, but does not have a eye tracking capability and nor a facial tracking capability. These are aspects that some industry experts have asked about and which in this case could have provided further info about the situation.

Why didn't the Tesla detect the attenuator?

In other words, even if the Tesla somehow was veering to the left, whether due to the human driver or due to the Autopilot itself, presumably the Autopilot should have still been able to detect that there was an attenuator up ahead and that the Tesla was heading straight for it.

There are a multitude of possibilities to explain this. It could be that on this sunny morning that the sun was in a position that caused glare and that the cameras on the Tesla could not get a clear enough image to detect the attenuator.

You might say that even if that happened, the forward-facing radar should have detected the attenuator. Was the attenuator so low to the ground and positioned that the radar couldn't get a solid radar return? Or, could it be that the damaged attenuator made it less likely to be spotted by radar?

Another possibility is that the camera was reporting that it didn't see anything ahead, and let's pretend the radar was saying there was something ahead, but suppose the AI system is coded in a manner that it needs to have both agree in order to take action. It might be that it was programmed that if the radar says be wary, but if the camera does not agree, then the car continues ahead and waits until the two will concur.

It is noteworthy too that the lead car was no longer ahead at the 4 second mark. This means that the time that the Tesla system had to presumably spot the attenuator was perhaps only with about 4 seconds left to go. To some degree, the camera images and the radar could have been blocked by the lead car. With the "sudden" appearance of the attenuator, there is another possible explanation for the situation.

One further scenario is that the Tesla system ran out of time.

Suppose that it really did get solid images of the attenuator, and that it got solid radar. The question arises as to how much time is needed by the Autopilot to digest this information and then take action.

Here's the standard framework of stages for a self-driving car:
- Sensor Data Collection
- Sensor Fusion Analysis
- Virtual World Model Updating
- AI Action Plan Updating
- Car Controls Commands

Suppose with 4 seconds left to impact, the sensor data collection took a chunk of that time. Then, assume that the sensor fusion of combining the sensor data took a chunk of that time, including maybe wrestling with a difference of opinion by the camera images versus the radar. Then, the virtual world model had to be updated to reflect the surroundings. Then, an AI action plan had to be updated as to what steps to next take in terms of the driving of the car. Finally, there is a chunk of time involved in issuing car controls commands and having the car respond and abide by the commands.

One aspect is that the Autopilot used up the available time and was in the midst of determining what to do. Perhaps it was going to take perhaps 5 seconds to figure out what to do and enact an evasive maneuver, but with just 4 seconds until impact it was too late by the time it figured out what action to take.

Awaiting the NTSB Final Report

Until the NTSB provides more details in subsequent reports about the incident, we're all in the dark about what actually happened.

In this analysis, I've opted to not get mired into the ongoing debate about who is responsible for the acts of a self-driving car in these kinds of incidents. As Tesla has made very clear, their view is that the human driver is ultimately responsible for the driving of the Tesla cars: "Autopilot is intended for use only with a fully attentive driver," furthermore it "does not prevent all accidents - such a standard would be impossible - but it makes them much less likely to occur."

For those of you that are interested in these kinds of self-driving car crash analyses, I'll be updating my analysis once there is more reporting by the NTSB about this incident. The end result will hopefully make us all aware of the potential limitations of self-driving cars and allow us all as a society to make further informed decisions about what we expect of them.

Copyright 2018 Dr. Lance Eliot

Chapter 8: AI in Canada -- Leadership Sets the Direction

Canada's AI Initiative Brings Together Government, Academia, Industry In Quest to Expand National Economy

Canada has emerged as a front-runner in AI development. The country has declared a national initiative around AI, pouring hundreds of millions of dollars into it and relaxing immigration rules to attract the best engineers.

Canada has a number of strengths that position the country well in AI, including a growing supply of Ph.D-level AI engineers in an era characterized by an acute global shortage of AI talent. This is largely due to leading universities in Toronto, Waterloo, Montreal and Edmonton that have invested heavily in AI research for years. "Canada now has one of the most significant concentrations of AI talent anywhere," stated Salim Teja, venture capitalist with MaRS, an innovation hub in Toronto, writing recently in Forbes.

Canadian Prime Minister Pierre Trudeau appeared at MIT's Solve event in May.

Graduates from Canada have gone on to lead labs in the world's top technology companies. They include: Geoffrey Hinton, VP and Engineering Fellow at the AI research team Google Brain, which also includes many other Canadians as senior researchers; Craig Boutilier, principal scientist at Google Research, which was recently renamed to Google AI; Alex Graves and Yujia Li, senior researchers at Google DeepMind, the AI research unit based in London, acquired by Google in 2014; Ilya Sutskever, co-founder and research director at Open AI, the non-profit AI research company that aims to promote "friendly AI;" Rusian Salakhutdinov, director of AI Research at Apple and a computer science professor at Carnegie

Mellon University; Yann LeCun, VP and Chief AI Scientist at Facebook; and Nebojsa Jojic, Principal Researcher at Microsoft Research.

Here are some recent developments:
- Vector Institute, a $170 million research center headed by Geoffrey Hinton (who some call the "godfather of AI") recently opened in Toronto. Hinton stated, "Increasingly, the world's most promising researchers in deep learning and other AI subfields at looking at Canada as a hub with many opportunities to collaborate."
- Geoffrey Gordon, a researcher at Carnegie Mellon University's machine learning department, recently announced he is moving to Montreal to lead its Microsoft Research Lab;
- Google's DeepMind, which developed the first software to defeat a human player in the strategy board game Go, has opened its first lab outside of the UK in Edmonton.
- Microsoft in early 2017 acquired Maluuba, a Montreal and Waterloo-based startup specializing in machine language understanding. Microsoft plans to double the size of the company's Montreal office by 2019.
- Tech Mahindra, an IT services firm based in India, announced in February 2018 it will invest $100 million in a Centre of Excellence in Toronto. The center plans to jointly develop business solutions in emerging technologies including AI with academic

institutes, innovators and accelerators in the Canadian startup ecosystem. Canada's Prime Minister Pierre Trudeau recently traveled to India to promote enhance bilateral collaboration between the two countries.

Canada also has vast amounts of data, by virtue of its publicly-funded systems in services including health, energy and transit. "These large datasets are goldminds for AI developers, not only because of their size but also because of their diversity," states Teja. Canadian diversity is a strength when it comes to address bias in AI datasets. In Toronto, more than 50% of the population is foreign-born.

Rather than trying to poach the best AI academics, startups and corporations in Canada are creating partnerships with universities that enable the researchers to stay involved in academia as well as industry. For example, the Royal Bank of Canada has created Borealis AI, a subsidiary that gives its staff latitude to collaborate with universities on research and jointly publish results.

In Montreal, Element AI is a venture founded by neural network pioneer Yoshua Bengio, working with University of Montreal (see recent AI Trends interview here) and McGill University researchers to jointly advance algorithms for companies looking to incorporate AI solutions into their business.

Canadian Government Investing, Startups Raising Money

PWC estimates that AI will add $19.4 trillion to the global economy by 2030. Canada sees AI as its biggest opportunity to expand its economy, alleviate its dependence on natural resources, evolve to new technology-driven industries and create a prosperous future, writes Steve Irvine recently in the Toronto Globe and Mail. Irvine in early 2017 left an executive role at Facebook to return to Canada and build integrate.ai, an AI-focused startup where he is the CEO.

In 2017, Canada invested more than $300 million in new funding for research and Canadian startups raised $260 million. In addition to DeepMind, global tech giants Facebook, Samsung and Uber have established AI research labs in Canada.

Canada faces competition for AI leadership. The US remains home to the world's leading AI companies including Google, Facebook, Apple, Amazon, many well-funded startups and strong universities including MIT, Stanford and Carnegie Mellon.

China plans to be a world AI leader by 2030; China recently committed $2.5 billion to a national AI research park in Beijing with a goal of supporting 400 companies producing revenue of $9.8 billion annually. With its own technology giants Alibaba, Tencent and Baidu, and its large population, China is well-positioned to capture a large share of the global AI market opportunity.

China seemed to mimic the Obama-era roadmap laid out in 2016 for AI leadership.

As the New York Times reported in February 2018, the Trump White House has been silent on a national AI strategy. 'We are still waiting on the White House to provide some direction" on how to respond to the competition, stated Tim Hwang, who worked at AI policy at Google and is now the director of the Ethics and Governance of AI Initiative, an organization created by LinkedIn founder Reid Hoffman and others to fund ethical research in AI.

Canada on the other hand is marshalling its national leadership to lead the charge. "It is essential that Canada shifts its focus more aggressively to commercialization from academic prowess," states Irvine. Canada today lacks the homegrown, global-leading technology companies that can capture the economic growth associated with the opportunity. "We need at least a handful of $10-billion-plus companies to help create the commercial density and global relevant needed to attract and retain elite talent, create new high-value jobs and capture economic gain," Irvine stated.

He encouraged Canadian businesses to commit to AI projects engaging startups to tackle meaningful business problems, to put strong people on it, and not tie them up for months with legal and procurement issues. "There is no better learning agenda for your team than rolling up their sleeve and seeing this new technology in practice delivering results for you," he states.

Focus on Montreal:
With its Academics, Culture of Collaboration, Access to Capital, Concern with Social Impact, Montreal Poised to be AI Startup Hotbed

With its confluence of academics, international accessibility, culture of collaboration, many startups and access to capital, Montreal may be poised to become the next Silicon Valley. This might be especially true given the current America political climate hostile to the international cooperation on which research institutions and technology companies thrive.
Montreal is benefitting today from a long-term commitment by the Canadian government to fund AI research.

"Canada has supported the fundamental basics of AI by financing Bengio (Yoshua Bengio, University of Montreal and MILA), LeCun (Yann LeCun, VP and Chief AI Scientist, Facebook) and Geoff Hinton (University of Toronto and Google), over 25 years, back to when AI was not as strong a bet " said Chris Arsenault, General Partner, iNovia Capital, Montreal, in an interview with AI Trends. "That's why Canada is in such a great position right now."

These scientists are a big pull for Canada to attract students and the many big technology companies who have opened research labs in Canada, especially in Montreal and Toronto. These include: IBM AI Lab; Facebook AI Center (FAIRE); Google AI Lab; Microsoft (acquired Maluuba in January 2017); Tencent, via an investment in Element.ai; Intel, also via Element.ai; Google DeepMind Center; Samsung AI Center; Thales Centre of Research & Tech in AI; the RBC (Royal Bank of Canada) Borealis AI Center; Uber AI; ADM AI lab (opening soon); NVIDIA, SunLife, Adobe; LG, Fujitsu; and TD (Toronto-Dominion Bank)/Layer 6.

"We are just starting to see the fruits of the results of all this research in the form of companies with business models and platforms incorporating AI," Arsenault said. Advances in chip design and availability of compute power via the cloud are also enabling the rush. "This was not possible five or 10 years ago," Arsenault added.

Companies Finding AI Talent in Montreal

A chief attraction for companies pursuing AI research and commercialization, is the access to top talent centered around the universities, in particularly the McGill University and the University of Montreal, which includes the Montreal Institute for Learning Algorithms (MILA), said to be one of the largest deep learning labs in the world. Partly this is due to the accomplishments of Dr. Bengio, one of the world's leading deep learning researchers.

"Montreal has the largest concentration of deep learning academics in the world. This attracts some of the best students, postdocs, professors, researchers, engineers and entrepreneurs interested in contributing to the ongoing AI revolution," Dr. Bengio stated.

The Canadian government's commitment to AI is exemplified in its support for MILA. The government of Quebec recently allocated $80 million over the near five years to support its growth, and the federal government's Pan-Canadian AI Strategy unit has granted MILA $44 million to supports its activities.

The MILA mission is to attract and retain talent in the machine learning field; to propel advanced research in deep learning and reinforcement learning; to transfer technology by supporting private AI startups and established businesses; and to contribute to the social dialogue and the development of applications that benefit society.

The new Facebook Artificial Intelligence Research (FAIR) in Montreal will be led by McGill University professor Joelle Pineau, a member of MILA. The plan is to employ research scientists and engineers engaged in a wide range of projects, with a focus on reinforcement learning and dialog systems. "Montreal already has an existing fantastic academic AI community, an exciting ecosystem of startups, and promising government policies to encourage AI research," stated LeCun in a press release about the investment. "We are excited to become part of this larger community, and we look forward to engaging with the entire ecosystem and helping it continue to thrive."

Joelle Pineau, head of Facebook FAIR lb in Toronto, professor at McGill University

"For many years, I have seen a steady stream of talented AI researchers with Masters and PhDs from our universities move to the US to find the best research jobs," Prof. Pineau stated in a release from McGill University. "They will now have an opportunity to do this right here in Montreal. The Montreal FAIR Lab will initially launch with ten researchers, with the aim of scaling up to more than 30 researchers in the coming year."

Technical talent in Montreal is attracted to companies who offer a chance to publish papers and "do something good for humanity," in the words of Patrick Poirier, chief technology of startup Erudite AI. "Trying to fight for talent with pure cash is a losing bet for startups in Montreal," he told Daniel Faggella, the founder of Tech Emergence, a market research company focused on AI and machine learning, who spent 12 days visiting AI related ventures and executives in Montreal last year and wrote an account of his conclusions.

Montreal Cost of Living, Diversity Are Strengths

The Montreal culture, lifestyle and relatively low cost of living compared to other urban tech centers such as San Francisco and Boston, is also attractive.

One technologist who made the move from Silicon Valley to Montreal is Maxime Chevalier-Boisvert, who returned to Montreal in mid-2017 after working at Apple for 13 months, according to an account in the New York Times. She had an opportunity to work with Yoshua Bengio at MILA and could not pass it up. Her title at MILA is Architect of Imaginary Machines. While her salary was about one-third of what she made at Apple, her rent for a two-bedroom apartment in Montreal was less than a third of the monthly rent she paid for a one-bedroom apartment in Sunnyvale. "Living in Montreal is pretty good," she stated.

The Montreal AI culture has also attracted investments from those concerned with the social impact and risks of AI. The Open Philanthropy Project in July 2017 awarded $2.4 million to MILA to support "technical research on potential risks from advanced AI," stated the announcement from OPP, which has a focus area on Global Catastrophic Risks that includes advanced AI. The OPP's two primary aims are to increase high-quality research on the safety of AI, and the number of people knowledgeable about both machine learning and the potential risks of AI.

Montreal's diversity of culture is also helping to attract talent. Dr. Alexandre Le Bouthillier, founder of machine vision healthcare company Imagia, observed that most talent in Montreal's AI community is foreign-born, with his own team coming from all over the globe. "Smart people know that talent attracts talent," he has stated.

Montreal and Toronto are benefitted from a Canadian immigration strategy consistent with the country's AI initiative. Canada launched a fast-track visa program for high-skilled workers in the summer of 2017. Today, foreign students make up 20 percent of all students at Canadian universities compared with less than five percent in the US, according to a recent [account in Politico](#) written by two University of Toronto professors, Richard Florida and Joshua Gans. Canadian immigration law also makes it easier for foreign students to remain in Canada after they graduate.

Since the election of Donald Trump as US president in November 2016, applications to Canadian universities have spiked upward. International student applications jumped 70 percent in the fall of 2017 compared to the previous year; applications to McGill University in Montreal jumped 30 percent; and those to the University of British Columbia in Vancouver increased by 25 percent, according to the authors.

Canadian Prime Minister Justin Trudeau views immigrants as contributing to the growth of the Canadian economy, particularly in areas of technical innovation. "People choosing to move to a new place are self-selected to be ambitious, forward-thinking, brave and builders of a better future," he stated in a recent account in TechCrunch. "For someone who chooses to do this to ensure their kids have a good life is a big step." The Canadian perspective on innovation is helping to attract talent not only for the opportunity to conduct technical research but also to study "the consequences of AI, the consequences of automation," Trudeau stated.

French culture has a big impact on Montreal, expanding beyond the delis and coffee shops and into business life. Many of the larger businesses primarily speak French in the office and in many of the top universities, including the University of Montreal.

Montreal Attracting Investment Capital

The ability of Montreal's universities and startups to attract capital from tech giants and investors has helped to cement its position. The ability of Montreal-based platform and incubator Element AI, to raise $102 million in a Series A round of investment in June 2017, was a tipping point. The firm's mission is to lower the barrier to entry for commercial applications in AI by offering AI talent and resources to companies that need to supplement their own staffs.

The round was led by Data Collective, which backs entrepreneurs applying deep learning technologies to transform giant industries, and included as partners Microsoft Ventures and NVIDIA. The Series A round came six months after Element AI announced a seed round from Microsoft Ventures (for an undisclosed amount) and eight months after the company launched.

The firm's approach is to build an "incubator" or "safe space" where companies that might sometimes compete, sit alongside each other and collaborate to build new products. Some believe this may be an industry first. Data Collective sees an opportunity to close the gap between the AI have and have-nots.

"There is not a lot left in the middle," Data Collective managing partner Matt Ocko told TechCrunch. "The issue with corporations, governments and others trapped in that no man's land of AI 'have-nots' is that their rivals with superior AI-powered decision making and signal processing will dominate global markets."

Element AI foresees initial product pickup in areas of: predictive modeling, forecasting models for small data sets, conversational AI and natural language processing, aggregation techniques based on machine learning, reinforcement learning for physics-based motion control, statistical machine learning algorithms, voice recognition, fluid simulation and consumer engagement optimization.

Element AI is not yet discussing customer engagements in depth, a spokesman told AI

Trends, but they have signed up as customers the Port of Montreal, Radio-Canada (Canadian media company) and the Canadian Space Agency. According to [a recent article in Fortune](), the company sees an opportunity to embed itself in large organizations that may use Google for email and Amazon for web services, but are reluctant to give those companies access to internal databases with company-sensitive information. Element AI sees an opportunity to position as a more ethical AI company than those involved with military contracts and election influencers.

The future looks good for AI innovation out of Montreal. Karam Thomas, founder and CEO of CognitiveChem, a company leveraging AI to help chemists develop safer chemicals, stated, "Montreal's unique advantage lies in its collaborative research between academia, startups and corporations." Montreal's AI boosters are hoping that collaboration will spur more entrepreneurs to build sizable new companies.

Chapter 9: AI at Google

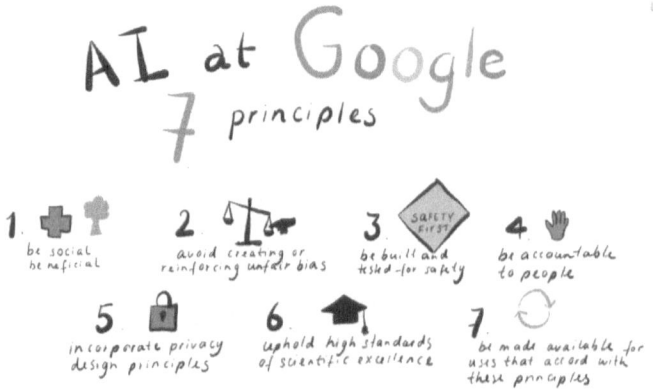

Credit: Illustration by Betty Feenstra

Google's Release of its AI Principles Sets a Bar

Google CEO Sundar Pichai released a set of AI principles for the company on June 7, 2018. He mentioned a project of high school students using AI-powered sensors to predict the risk of wildfires. He mentioned Google's investments in the use of AI to help diagnose cancer.

He also said Google will not deploy AI in weapons systems primarily meant to harm people. This announcement followed by days Google's decision to not renew its contract to participate with the US Department of Defense on Project Maven to develop intelligent drones. Google's role was to use AI to help analyze video footage from the drones.

The contract was said to be worth hundreds of millions of dollars, and would likely have led to a cloud computing contract worth billions down the road, according to an account in VentureBeat.

Google's involvement in Maven led to an employee revolt. Google Cloud chief scientist Dr.Fei-Fei Li wrote in emails obtained by the New York Times, "Weaponized AI is probably one of the most sensitized topics of AI -- if not THE most. This is read meat to the media to find all ways to damage Google."

About a dozen Google employees resigned in protest; more than 3,000 signed letters starting that Google should not participate in the creation of autonomous weaponry.

In October, CEO Pichai met quietly with Pentagon officials in Washington in an effort to smooth the relationship, and to help keep the company in position to win Defense Department contracts. Google's change of heart over Project Maven has become a key source of tension between the tech giant and military officials, according to an account in the Washington Post. The military officials felt

Google could have done a better job communicating that the technology could help keep military personnel out of harm's way.

"Without a doubt, this has caused a lot of consternation inside the DOD," said Bob Work, the former deputy secretary of defense who helped launch Project Maven last year, to the Post. "Google created a big moral hazard for itself by saying it doesn't want to use any of its AI technology to take human life. But they didn't say anything about the lives that could be saved."

US Being Outpaced in Race for Global AI Leadership

Elsewhere, Google received credit for releasing its AI Principles. The US is being outpaced in the global race for AI Leadership, suggested writers of a piece in The National Review in July. China has committed $150 billion to focused AI research spending; Canada got its start 25 years ago with the support of its government; France has committed $2B to AI applied research. The US needs an AI strategy.

In the absence of this, Google seeks to establish its own guidelines, which naturally align with its corporate self-interest. And while Google's AI principles may offer a glimpse into what a national AI strategy could be, they may not align with the national interest, the National Review authors suggest.

Meanwhile, Google rankings consistently elevate conspiracy theories that hurt democracies around the world, and that videos on its YouTube unit are used to spread propaganda and incite violence. "In short, AI is already weaponized in the current environment," the authors state. Google's definition of weapons is confined to hardware, an unmanned system, while its products are used for information warfare. Smart government policy is needed to reach a better understanding on security.

The private sector will be critical to the establishment of a comprehensive AI strategy. "Google CEO Sundar Pichai should be lauded for his leadership in highlighting this fap, but the private sector should not be the sole entity that is articulating and implementing a national AI strategy," suggest the authors. (*The authors were Evanna Hu, CEO of Omelas, a machine learning company, and Stephen Rodriguez, founder of One Defense and a visiting professor at the Naval Postgraduate School.*)

Dragonfly Chinese Search Engine Project Raises Questions

Reports surfaced in early August that Google was working on a project call Dragonfly, to launch a mobile search app that would censor results in compliance with the Chinese government. Google had pulled its servers from mainland China in 2010 over concerns with the government's censorship. And Google's cloud division is said to be in talks with multiple Chinese companies about partnerships, Bloomberg reported.

According to a transcript of an employee meeting obtained by Bloomberg, Pichai said, "China is one-fifth of the world's population. I think if we were to do our mission well, I think we have to think seriously about how we do more in China."

Coming after its decision to pull out of the US DOD project, this did not go over well in the US Congress. At a hearing in September at which

Google executives declined to appear, Republican Senator Tom Cotton of Arkansas was critical of Google for working with Chinese companies while withdrawing from a partnership with the US DOD. Pichai was expected to appear at a hearing in Washington in the fall.

Google of course was not confined to political entanglements in 2018. In September, Google's DeepMind unit announced "near human performance" on CT scans of patients with cancer of the head and neck, according to an account in VentureBeat. The scans are used to isolate areas of skin to receive radiotherapy treatment, a delicate process. DeepMind partnered with University College London Hospital on the segmentation project.

"Automated ... segmentation has the potential to address these challenges but, to date, performance of available solutions in clinical practice has proven inferior to that of expert human operators," the researchers wrote. "In recent years, deep learning based algorithms have proven capable of delivering substantially better performance than traditional segmentation algorithms."

In a presentation at the Medical Image Computing & Computer Assisted Intervention conference, the DeepMind team described a three-dimensional U-Net architecture trained with 663 tomography scans of 21 organs (larynx, tongue, nasal cavity, connective and soft tissue) sourced from head and neck cancer patients at the University College London Hospitals NHS Foundation Trust (UCLH). Training took less than 30 seconds on a single GPU, they noted. Expert humans need to spend hours to make similar findings.

Further testing showed no substantial gap between results obtained by the model and radiographers on any individual patient. The next phase of research for the project will be to test the AI system's performance in a clinical environment. The team believes it has the potential to reduce the lag time between diagnosis and treatment, and to cut down on the time it takes to adapt procedures as the tumor shrinks, a process known as adaptive radiotherapy.

"Increasing demands for and shortages of trained staff already place a heavy burden on healthcare systems, which can lead to long delays for patients as radiotherapy is planned," they wrote. "As well as changing patients' lives, this research could also free up time for the clinicians who treat them, meaning they get to spend more time on patient care, education and research."

DeepMind is involved in several other health-related AI projects, including an ongoing trial at the U.S. Department of Veterans Affairs that seeks to predict when patients' conditions will deteriorate during a hospital stay. Previously, it partnered with the U.K.'s National Health Service to develop an algorithm that could search for early signs of blindness, and to improve breast cancer detection by applying machine learning to mammography.

New York University Lung Cancer Advance with Google's Deep Learning

Another healthcare win for Google came from research published in September in Nature Medicine, describing a project of scientists at New York University, who retrained an off-the-shelf Google deep learning algorithm to distinguish between two common types of lung cancer with 97 percent accuracy. This image recognition AI, the same technology that identifies faces, animals and objects in pictures uploaded to Google, has proven to be effective in diagnosing disease including diabetic blindness and heart conditions. But the NYU neural network learned to do something new that no pathologist had done before, identify the genetic mutations inside each tumor from a picture.

"I thought the real novelty would be not just to show the AI is as good as humans, but to have it provide insights a human expert would not be able to," says Aristotelis Tsirigos, a pathologist at the NYU School of Medicine and a lead author on the new study, as quoted in an account in Wired.

To do so, Tsirigos' team started with Google's Inception v3—an open-source algorithm that Google trained to identify 1,000 different classes of objects. To teach the algorithm to distinguish between images of cancerous and healthy tissue, the researchers showed it hundreds of thousands of images taken from The Cancer Genome Atlas, a public library of patient tissue samples.

Once Inception figured out how to pick out cancerous cells with 99 percent accuracy, the next step was teaching it to tell two kinds of lung cancers apart—adenocarcinoma from squamous cell carcinoma. Together, they represent the most prevalent forms of the disease, which kills more than 150,000 people a year. While they appear similar under the microscope, the two cancer types are treated very differently. Getting it right can mean the difference between life and death for patients.

When the researchers tested Inception on independent samples taken from cancer patients at NYU, its accuracy went down a bit, but not much. It still correctly diagnosed the images between 83 and 97 percent of the time. That's not surprising, says Tsirigos, given that the hospital's samples carried much more noise—inflammation, dead tissue, and white blood cells—and were often processed differently than the frozen TCGA samples. Improving the accuracy will just be a matter of having pathologists annotate slides with more of those additional features, so the algorithm can learn to pick those out too.

But it wasn't a helping human hand that taught Inception to 'see' genetic mutations in those histology slides. That trick the algorithm learned all on its own.

Again working with data from the TCGA, Tsirigos' team fed Inception genetic profiles for each tumor, along with the slide images. When they tested their system on new images, it was able to not only identify which ones showed cancerous tissue, but the genetic mutations of that particular tissue sample. The neural network had learned to notice extremely subtle changes to a tumor sample's appearance, which pathologists cannot see. "These cancer-driving mutations appear to have microscopic effects that the algorithm can detect," said Tsirigos to Wired. What those subtle changes are, however, "we don't know. They're buried [in the algorithm] and nobody really knows how to extract them."

In the coming months, the NYU researchers will keep training their AI program with more data from more varied sources. Then they'll start thinking about spinning up a company to seek FDA approval. Because of cost and time, sequencing of tumor samples isn't always the standard of care in the US. Imagine being able to send in a digital photo of a tumor sample and get a diagnosis complete with viable treatment options almost instantaneously. That's where this is all headed, the Wired authors suggested.

"The big question is, will this be trustworthy enough to replace current practice?" says Daniel Rubin, Director of Biomedical Informatics at the Stanford Cancer Institute. Not without a lot of future validation work, he says. But it does point toward a future where pathologists work in partnership with computers. "What this paper really shows is that there's a lot more information in the images than what a human being can pull out."

With Google and other companies making state-of-the-art algorithms available as open-source code, researchers can now start an AI project of their own with relative ease. With just a bit of customization, those neural nets are ready to be set loose on a mountain of biomedical image data, not just tumor images.

Financial Reports on DeepMind Show Rising Expenses

The good news coming out of Google's DeepMind investment was tempered a bit in October, when internal financial reports documented increasing costs for DeepMind. According to an account in Business Insider, DeepMind saw its costs almost triple in 2017, due to rising staff and infrastructure investments.The reports were filed at the UK's Companies House.

The key numbers reported for the year to December 2017:

- **Revenue**: £54.4 million ($71 million), up 35% from £40.3 million ($52 million) in 2016.
- **Losses before tax**: £281.9 million ($366 million), up 123% from £126.6 million ($164 million) in 2016.
- **Expenses**: £333.8 million ($433 million), up 104% from £164 million ($213 million).
- **Staff costs**: £200 million ($260 million), up 91% from £104.7 million ($136 million) in 2016.

Google acquired the UK-based business for £400 million (then $600 million) in 2014, in a major bet on the future of artificial intelligence. The company has made history in its mission to create general artificial intelligence. In 2016, its AlphaGo algorithm beat the world's human champion at the strategy game Go, one of the most difficult games ever invented.

Last year, the firm attracted controversy for its work in healthcare, with the UK's data watchdog finding that its data-sharing deal with the Royal Free hospital was illegal. It has tried to move past that scandal and is cementing more clinical partnerships and healthcare research projects. In August (2018), the firm unveiled research showing its AI could detect eye disease.

Staff costs almost doubled to £200 million. That figure covers salaries as well as benefits and costs like pensions and travel. Staff numbers were not reported in its earnings, which is relatively unusual, but CEO Demis Hassabis said in 2017 the firm had about 700 employees.

DeepMind's revenue doesn't, as yet, reflect any money it makes from its healthcare work. A spokeswoman said its reported turnover mostly reflects the work DeepMind does for its parent Google, such as using AI to cool Google's server warehouses and work on Google Assistant.

According to a June report by a panel that oversees the firm's healthcare work, the company doesn't make money from its health business yet.

The filings show DeepMind spent £8.1 million on academic donations. Asked for clarification, a spokeswoman said the company had given grants to New York University, University College London, Imperial, and the University of Alberta "to support AI research initiatives." The donations don't come with conditions, she added, and all institutions disclose their grants publicly.

In March 2018, Google announced a new cloud service that converts blocks of text into natural-sounding speech, the first product containing DeepMind code that was for sale. The new Google

Cloud Text-to-Speech application programming interface costs $16 for every million characters of text it processes in DeepMind's artificial male and female voices, according to a report on CNBC.

On an earnings call in 2016, an analyst from Sanford Bernstein asked about DeepMind as a financial driver. Google CEO Sundar Pichai responded, "Looking at the pace of progress, I think we will have AI in a form in which it benefits a lot of users in the coming years, but I still think it's early days, and there's a long-term investment for us."

Chapter 10: AI at Amazon

This announcement was made in 2016.

Focus on AI Helping Amazon Make AWS Center of Tech Universe

Amazon reached a trillion dollar market capitalization in early September, five weeks after Apple, the first company to accomplish the feat.

Analysts cited the company's diversified portfolio as a driver, noting its launch into the grocery industry with the purchase of Whole Foods in 2017. In the tech world, Amazon has impressed with the growth of Amazon Web Services, which grew 50 percent in Q2 2018.

RBC Capital Markets analyst Mark Mahaney told CNBC, "Yes, Amazon did really well in online retail, but then the stock gapped up when they showed that they could become successful in cloud. It's almost like the ticker changed from AMZN to AWS."

Amazon Web Services is offering a path to AI for many companies. One example is the Chick-fil-A restaurant chain, which is using AWS to explore how AI can help its business. Kesha Williams, a software engineering manager in the Information Technology department at Chick-fil-A, told *AI Trends* in an interview that the innovative cloud service has been crucial.

"Before the advent of cloud services like Amazon Web Services, I would've said, yes, there's a lot lacking in the industry as far as support for AI. But now, thanks to AWS services like Amazon Machine Learning, Amazon Rekognition, which is their computer vision service, and Amazon Alexa Skills Kit, we're now able to quickly build prototypes to help prove out the feasibility of our innovative ideas." she said. "There are so many opportunities to provide innovative solutions to the industry thanks to services like AWS."

Amazon has arguably rewired the entire company around AI. CEO Jeff Bezos in 2014 was asking for "six pagers" -- his legendary format for new product and service proposals, which include a press release at the end announcing the innovation -- about how AI could transform whatever unit of the company the presenter represented.

One of the presenters was Srikanth Thirumalai, the head of Amazon's recommendation team, a computer scientist who had left IBM in 2005. He proposed a sweeping new plan to incorporate the latest advances in AI into his division. Amazon had relied on AI for its recommendations, and robots in its shipping warehouses for years, but Bezos was looking for a company-wide transformation that exploited recent gains in AI research.

Thirumalai was one of many company leaders who presented Bezos with variations on the theme of using AI to transform their business units.

"We went out to every [team] leader, to basically say, 'How can you use these techniques and embed them into your own businesses?'" says David Limp, Amazon's VP of devices and services, quoted in an account in Wired.

At the time, Amazon's AI expertise was in pockets throughout the company.

"We would talk, we would have conversations, but we wouldn't share a lot of artifacts with each other because the lessons were not easily or directly transferable," Thirumalai told Wired.

Internal Collaboration Has Led to Innovations

Collaboration across projects began taking place to connect the AI islands. Machine learning innovations in one part of the company began benefitting other teams Then the machine learning platforms began to be offered to the outside world via AWS, to the benefit of companies such as Chick-fil-A.

The Amazon recommendation system has become smarter as a result. Thirumalai is now head of Amazon Search, where he intends to further the use of deep learning techniques.

"If you asked me seven or eight years ago how big a force Amazon was in AI, I would have said, 'They aren't,'" said Pedro Domingos, a top computer science professor at the University of Washington, to Wired. "But they have really come on aggressively. Now they are becoming a force."

Amazon had difficulty attracting leading AI researchers from academia, largely owing to its culture of secrecy and relentless focus on only researching what would benefit customers. It has managed to attract some scientists who find the challenge of working on hard problems to be irresistible.

A project to develop a more conversational AI for the Alexa voice-activated assistant is one example. Amazon recruited Rohit Prasad, a speech recognition scientist at Raytheon BBN in Boston. He told Wired, "It was green fields here. Google and Microsoft had been working on speech for years. At Amazon we could build from scratch and solve hard problems." He was put on the Alexa project when he joined in 2013. "The device existed in terms of the hardware, but it was very early in speech," he said.

It's come a long way. Today when you speak into your Alexa device, you can access Amazon Music,

Prime Video, your personal recommendations from the main shipping website, and other services.

Amazon is amassing a trove of data from how people are using its voice-activated services, and that data is helping the company to attract more AI experts.

"One of the things that made Alexa so attractive to me is that once you have a device in the market, you have the resource of feedback. Not only the customer feedback, but the actual data that is so fundamental to improving everything—especially the underlying platform," said Ravi Jain, an Alexa VP of machine learning who joined the company last year, to Wired.

The extension of AWS into AI services was the brainchild of Swami Sivasubramanian, who was managing the AWS database and analytics business in 2014, when he began to be fascinated by the potential of machine learning. Making it easy to run machine-learning algorithms in the cloud, like Kesha Williams of Chick-fil-A is now doing, would appeal to developers.

"We cater to millions of developers every month," he told Wired. "The majority are not professors at MIT but developers who have no background in machine learning."

That six-pager was a blueprint for how AWS could become the center of machine-learning activity throughout the technical community. Amazon

Machine Learning was first offered in 2015. New offerings in 2016 extended into text-to-speech, natural language processing and vision.

As companies build machine learning applications using AWS, it is less likely they will move to competing cloud services from Google, Microsoft or IBM. And the more companies that use AWS for AI, the more advantage Amazon gains.

"It's like Willie Sutton saying he robs banks because that's where the money is," said DigitalGlobe CTO Walter Scott to Wired about why his firm uses Amazon's technology. "We use AWS for machine learning because that's where our customers are."

The expansion of cloud services and the increased spending on cloud services is giving rise to optimization businesses. A Business Insider report maintains that companies was $62 billion annually in the cloud by paying for capacity they don't need. One company positioning to help is CloudSqueeze, an AWS partner, which aims to simplify cloud deployment with AI, and help companies not waste money in the cloud.

In About Us on its website, CloudSqueeze states, "We have created an intelligent platform that enables decision-makers to get timely alerts to eliminate wasted spend, get actionable insights, prevent budget overruns with proactive change, utilization, prediction of cloud intelligence."

The use of AI to manage AI is no doubt unavoidable.

Chapter 11: AI at Facebook

Facebook CEO Mark Zuckerberg hopes AI can help solve his fake news challenge.

As Facebook Hires More AI Scientists, Its Fake News Challenge Persists

Facebook is working on doubling the size of its Facebook Artificial Intelligence Research (FAIR) division in the next two years, from the current staff of 180 to 200, to almost 400 by 2020 as Facebook works to put AI at the core of its platforms.

"I don't know everybody's name anymore and I don't recognise everybody either," said Facebook's chief AI scientist, Yann LeCun, in an interview in Forbes.

Some of research conducted at FAIR is applied to Facebook platforms such as Instagram and Whatsapp, by an applied machine learning team and other engineers, but must of the research is purely academic.

Competition for AI talent is intense, with Facebook, Google, Apple, Amazon and Microsoft vying for the best PhD students and other academics.

Facebook is using a "co-employment model" where its new hires from universities retain part-time academic positions.

"This dual affiliation model is common across FAIR, with many of our researchers around the world splitting their time between FAIR and a university," wrote LeCun, chief AI scientist at Facebook, in a blog post announcing the news.

LeCun added: "This model allows people within FAIR to continue teaching classes and advising graduate students and postdoctoral researchers, while publishing papers regularly. This co-employment appointment concept is similar to how many professors in medicine, law, and business operate."

Carnegie Mellon University's Jessica Hodgins, a professor of robotics and computer science, will lead the new Facebook AI lab in Pittsburgh, where she will be joined by Abhinav Gupta, an associate professor of robotics at Carnegie Mellon University. The Pittsburgh lab will focus on robotics, lifelong learning systems that learn continuously over the years and AI in support of creativity.

Prof. Hodgins research focuses on computer graphics, animation and robotics, with an emphasis on generating and analyzing human motion. Gupta will focus on large-scale visual and robot learning, self-supervised learning and reasoning. Both retain their Carnegie Mellon positions part-time.

Luke Zettlemoyer, associate professor at the Paul G. Allen School of Computer Science & Engineering at the University of Washington, Seattle, was hired in 2018 in the Seattle office, where the AI Research and Computational Photography teams are located. He has expertise in natural language processing, and his research will focus on computational semantics, including deep learning methods for multilingual language understanding, according to LeCun.

In London, Oxford's Andrea Vedaldi, an associate professor of engineering science, will join Facebook and focus on computer vision and machine learning. He retains his position of associate professor of engineering science with the University of Oxford, where he also co-leads the Visual Geometry Group. For Facebook, he will be researching image understanding, specifically on unsupervised learning through large and diverse visual datasets, and understanding geometric 3D reasoning, according to LeCun.

Facebook is also supporting selected students at the University of Oxford through PhD scholarships.

Also joining Facebook in London is the team behind Bloomsbury AI, which Facebook acquired in June for an estimated $23 million to $30 million, reported TechCrunch. Bloomsbury, founded in 2015, had been working on natural language processing. They will continue to pursue research in text understanding and reasoning systems, according to LeCun.

In Menlo Park, researcher Jitendra Malik, known for his work in computer vision, recently joined from UC Berkeley. He retains a part-time position with UC Berkeley; the Berkeley AI Research Lab is receiving funding from FAIR.

LeCun is a French-born computer scientist who has worked primarily in the fields of machine learning, computer vision, mobile robotics and computational neuroscience. He was a postdoctoral research associate in Geoffrey Hinton's lab at the University of Toronto from 1987 to 1988. (Hinton is called by some the "Godfather of Deep Learning" for his work on a backpropagation algorithm for training multilayer neural networks. He now divides his time between Google and the University of Toronto.)

LeCun, while working at AT&T Bell Laboratories in Holmdel, New Jersey, developed new machine learning methods including a biologically-inspired model of image recognition called Convolutional Neural Networks. This was applied to an optical character recognition system used by NCR and other companies, that at one point in the late 1990s and early 2000s read 10% of all checks in the US.

In 2013, LeCun founded the International Conference on Learning Representations with Yoshua Bengio, the Canadian computer scientist noted for his work on artificial neural networks and deep learning.

LeCun joined Facebook about five years ago, and became Chief AI Officer in March 2018.

Facebook has many areas where it could use help from AI.

For example, Facebook Live, which launched in 2014, has been used to broadcast violent acts.

"There is some negativity around Facebook Live and being able to manage that," Facebook Chief Global Security Officer Nick Lovrien told CIO. "We're continuing to work with AI to solve those."

In an appearance before Congress in April 2018, Facebook founder and CEO Mark Zuckerberg pledged that automated tools would help solve some of the company's most challenging problems, including extremist propaganda, misinformation and hate speech. While AI has boosted the company's ability to monitor its two billion users, it still needs to rely on human moderators for much of the work.

LeCun was quoted in The Washington Post as saying that AI "works not so well with false news."

The reality of Facebook's problems with fake news became understood after the election of Donald Trump as US President in November 2016. Fake news stories were carefully placed on Facebook to incite voters and exploit divisions. Research showed that the fake stories were shared more than real ones. This was a year when the news consumption habits of Americans were such at two-third of citizens were getting news from social media platforms that did not employ editors or fact checkers.

Facebook at first denied or could not believe that fake news could have influenced voting decisions, but later Zuckerberg and COO Sheryl Sandberg embarked on an apology tour. The company had always maintained that it is a technology platform and not a media organization. "Facebook stumbled into the news business without systems, editorial frameworks and editorial guidelines, and now it's trying to course-correct," said Clair Wardle, research director at the Tow Center for Digital Journalism, in a 2016 interview with The Guardian.

Many are skeptical that Facebook can solve its fake news problem with AI.

"Facebook will be used as a weaponized propaganda platform as long as its users keep clicking. Mark Zuckerberg, I'm sure, never saw in 2004 that his site might be hijacked for such a purpose, but here we are," wrote Mark Sullivan in Fast Company in July 2018.

Facebook will make an effort. The company announced in July that it had hired some 7,500 human moderators. In a March interview with the New York Times, Zuckerberg said the company "deployed some new AI tools to identify fake accounts and false news" before a special election on Alabama. The company later clarified that it had deployed machine learning to find "suspicious behaviors without assessing the content itself."

Writing in The Verge in April 2018, writer James Vincent stated, "The challenges of building an automated fake news filter with artificial intelligence are numerous. From a technical perspective, AI fails on a number of levels because it just can't understand human writing the way humans do. It can pull out certain facts and do a crude sentiment analysis (guessing whether a piece of content is "happy" or "angry" based on keywords), but it can't understand subtleties of tone, consider cultural context, or ring someone up to corroborate information. And even if it could do all this, which would knock out the most obvious misinformation and hoaxes, it would eventually run up against edge cases that confuse even humans. If people on the left and the right can't agree on what is and is not "fake news," there's no way we can teach a machine to make that judgement for us."

The Fake News Challenge competition was an effort in 2017 to crowdsource machine learning solutions to identify fake news. Dean Pomerleau of Carnegie Mellon University, who helped organize the challenge, told The Verge that his team concluded that AI could not tackle the problem alone. "We actually started out with a more ambitious goal of creating a system that could answer the question 'Is this fake news, yes or no?' We quickly realized machine learning just wasn't up to the task," Pomerleau stated. Comprehension was a primary problem.

The many newly-hired accomplished AI scientists now working at Facebook, may find ways to curb the use of Facebook as a fake news platform. The challenge is before them; we shall see.

Chapter 12: AI at Microsoft

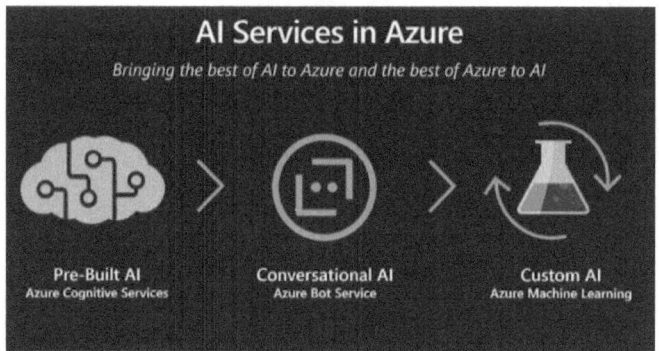

AI Services in Azure

Successful Advances into Cloud Services, AI and Windows Maturity

Microsoft announced a reorganization in March that marked the end of an era for Windows and a continued march toward cloud computing services and AI as the future of the company.

The move furthered the strategy of CEO Satya Nadella, appointed in 2014, to move toward faster-growing businesses. In an email to employees, Nadella outlined the reason for the changes and new executive appointments. He said in part, "AI capabilities are rapidly advancing across perception and cognition fueled by data and knowledge of the world."

The move was an acknowledgement that cloud services from Amazon, Microsoft and Google have become the internet equivalent of Windows, which had been the dominant operating system of the personal computing era.

The reorganization is "really doubling down on the cloud as the fundamental platform for Microsoft," said Ed Anderson, an analyst at Gartner, quoted in The New York Times.

Microsoft's cloud business has grown dramatically. In early 2018, Microsoft reported its Azure cloud computing service business grew 98 percent and its cloud-based Office 365 offering by 41 percent. By contrast, the division that includes the Windows PC software increased two percent.

When fiscal 2018 results were announced in July, Azure had grown 89 percent year over year, driving revenue growth for the server and cloud division 26 percent. While Amazon Web Services held the cloud computing market lead, Microsoft is cementing its position as a strong second, followed by Google. Microsoft's overall revenue had grown to over $100 billion for the first time.

Nadella stated about the results, "Our early investments in the intelligent cloud and intelligent edge are paying off, and we will continue to expand our reach in large and growing markets with differentiated innovation."

On an earnings call with investors reported by The Guardian, Nadella attributed the strong results in part to the recent reorganization of the company's engineering teams to prioritize cloud computing and artificial intelligence over its legacy software products and Windows operating system.

Microsoft Gets a Win with Walmart

On the earnings call, Nadella said he was "especially proud" of a new five-year deal between Microsoft and Walmart, which has been widely described as a strategic alliance against Amazon.

Announced during the Amazon Prime Day sale, the deal will see Walmart shift a significant portion of walmart.com and samsclub.com to Azure, Microsoft's cloud business.

"Walmart was never going to partner with Amazon for obvious reasons and Microsoft is the second largest provider of cloud solutions in the world," said Dusan Milosavljevic, an analyst at Berenberg bank, quoted in CNN Business.

Walmart will also get access to AI technology that could reduce energy consumption in its stores and machine learning expertise that would improve its delivery systems.

Microsoft also announced in June the $7.5 billion acquisition of GitHub, the code-sharing site at the heart of the open source tech world. Nadella spoke of the "increasingly vital role the developers play" and the opportunity through GitHub to "bring our tools and services to a new audience,".reported the Times.

Entering the AI Ethics Arena

In the reorganization announced in March, Nadella also said Microsoft's research leader, Harry Shum, and president, Brad Smith, have established a panel, the A.I. and Ethics in Engineering and Research Committee, to increase the odds that A.I. technology "benefits the broader society."

That move, said Patrick Moorhead, an independent analyst, is Microsoft's effort to show it is "serious about the broader implications of A.I." at a time of rising concern about the technology's influence on people's behavior and as a threat to jobs, the Times reported.

The Microsoft ethics group surely has its hands full after the announcement by Microsoft in late October that the company will bid on the

Department of Defense's $10 billion single-source cloud deal called JEDI - for Joint Enterprise Defense Infrastructure.

The tech giants have been thrashing over how closely to work with the Pentagon, especially around AI. After an uprising of Google employees, Google announced it would exit the JEDI competition. Google had announced a set of AI principles in 2018, and the company said it was not sure the defense would align with those principles. Google has an estimated 10% of cloud services market share.

Microsoft has not such qualms, despite its newly-formed ethics group. An Oct. 26 blog post by Microsoft president Brad Smith defended the company's relationship with the Department of Defense, which goes back four decades, and at the same time said the work would put Microsoft at the forefront of conversations about the ethical use of AI in warfare.

"We want the people of this country and especially the people who serve this country to know that we at Microsoft have their backs," Smith wrote. "They will have access to the best technology that we create."

That post came in response to a an open letter to the company from an unidentified group of Microsoft employees, reported by FCW which tracks federal technology purchasing, that urged the company not to bid on JEDI, out of concerns about the lethal applications of AI.

"If Microsoft is to be accountable for the products and services it makes, we need clear ethical guidelines and meaningful accountability governing how we determine which uses of our technology are acceptable, and which are off the table," the employees wrote in the open letter.

The bid process for JEDI has attracted protests from Oracle, which alleges that the procurement is built for a single vendor, and by IBM. Members of Congress are quizzing the DOD Inspector General on how the final set of requirements for the single-cloud project was determined. This dispute is likely to continue and the overall debate about AI warfare is likely to intensify.

Meanwhile Windows, still the most popular operating system for desktops and laptops, spreads to more form factors and remains a core Microsoft platform.

Chapter 13: Executive Interview: Kesha Williams, Chick-fil-A

Incorporating AI, Innovation To Meet Business Objectives, With Help from Amazon AWS

Kesha Williams is a software engineering manager in the Information Technology department at Chick-fil-A, the restaurant chain, with responsibility to lead and mentor junior software engineers and deliver new and innovative technology capabilities. She has worked in IT for over 20 years; she started at Chick-fil-A 13 years ago, working on a range of projects including build outs of Web applications used

Kesha Williams of Chick-fil-A

internally and by franchise owners. She is a graduate of Spelman College in Atlanta, computer science major. She recently took some time to talk to AI Trends Editor John P. Desmond.

Q. Can you tell us about your role in information technology at Chick-fil-A?

A. I've been with Chick-fil-A for the last 13 years, and I've worn many hats during my time there. In my current role, I serve as a software engineering manager; that entails many things. First, I'm responsible for just leading and mentoring junior software engineers. I also help to define and implement the onboarding process for our new engineers. And I develop technical training curriculum to keep all of our engineers up to speed on the latest and greatest technologies. And then I'm also able to code and build solutions that use Angular, Java, Spring and Amazon Web Services.

And in a really fun part of my role, I lead innovation teams. We investigate emerging technologies like artificial intelligence, machine learning, computer vision, virtual and augmented reality, and voice-first technology. I lead teams investigating how we can use these technologies to help move the business forward. And then, lastly, I serve as what we call a technical evangelist for Chick-fil-A, so I speak at conferences on Chick-fil-A's behalf and share some of the cool and exciting things we do in IT. So that's my role. Yeah, it's a lot. It's a lot of fun, too.

Q. It sounds like a really interesting job. Where does AI fall on the strategic roadmap of Chick-fil-A? And how would you describe the degree of support for AI technology investigation from the top management at the company?

A. From an IT perspective, we exist to power the promise of the brand, so top management and IT work together to foster a culture of innovation. IT is responsible for delivering new technology capabilities to enable business success. We are encouraged to innovate and think outside of the box when we are trying to solve business problems. And of our top five projects for this year, three of them have an AI component, either directly or indirectly. So we definitely see AI as a technology that will help us deliver new capabilities to the business.

Q. Can you talk about what AI technologies you are exploring for the company and/or could you talk about any of the projects that incorporate AI that you're working on?

A. I can speak at a high level about some of the AI technologies that we are exploring. We are exploring machine learning, computer vision and facial recognition, and voice-first virtual assistants. One of the innovation teams that I led won the Think Different Innovation Award from Chick-fil-A for thinking outside of the box in developing Amazon Alexa skills, for use by Operators in the restaurant and by customers outside of the restaurant.

And we've explored machine learning to assist with making reward and "treat" recommendations via our Chick-fil-A One Mobile app.

Q. Can you talk about what the virtual or augmented reality could be used for?

A. We have a Chick-fil-A One mobile app, and we're always seeking ways to have customers engage with mobile and online ordering. We've discussed that augmented reality could be a way to gamify the mobile ordering app. So, for example, we have the Chick-fil-A Cow Calendars. Each month, there is a free treat that you can redeem at your local Chick-fil-A restaurant. But there are some months where we have mystery items, so a customer will not know what the free treat is until that month.

We've discussed that augmented reality could be a way to gamify the Chick-fil-A One mobile app so customers can hold their phone up over the calendar, and see the mystery item revealed on the screen. The customer might see a chicken sandwich or a milkshake pop up in place of the mystery item. It's a fun way to engage customers to encourage ordering through the mobile app.

Q. Could you talk about how you got started in software engineering yourself?

A. I've been in IT for about 23 years, and I've been coding and building apps since high school. At the time, I didn't realize it was called coding. I just called it playing with the computer. My father purchased a personal computer for our home when I was in high school, and he placed it in my playroom. So we had this room that was a playroom/office, and I just always joked with people and say I had a Barbie doll in one hand and the computer manual in the other hand writing code using the BASIC programming language.

I've just always loved computers and technology. And because I was exposed to coding at such an early age, when it was time for me to decide what I was going to do with my life, and decide on a college major, it was easy for me to pick computer science and mathematics. Then after a summer internship with the NSA, I knew that I'd made the right decision. It's been full speed ahead since then.

Q. You like to work with students, guiding them as interns at the start of their careers. What advice would you have for young people pursuing a career either in AI, if they're interested in that, or IT, or what kind of exposure they need, what kind of experience? And, if they're in school, what should they study?

A. I would definitely recommend having computer programming as a baseline. That's what I learned when I was at Spelman College. I learned all the different concepts needed to build and write computer programs. It's a solid foundation. That knowledge can be transferred to all the different areas in IT.

Specifically for students that want to pursue AI, I would recommend learning the Python programming language. I also see voice-first technology and virtual assistants as an easy entry point to AI because it's so easy to get started, and you can quickly build and develop solutions that can be in the hands of millions of users in a very short period of time. So you receive instant gratification and feedback. That's what I would recommend.

Q. Chick-fil-A is a big company, with many franchise owners. How does the pursuit of innovative technologies, including AI, fit within the whole organization?

A. In IT, we pursue innovation because it's our job to deliver new technology capabilities that enable business success. So innovation is weaved into everything we do. For example, once a quarter we have an Innovation Day. This is where we are able to step outside of our day to day routine, our day to day job, and tinker with emerging technologies, mostly AI, to see how we can improve restaurant operations and customer experiences inside and outside of the restaurant. Through the Innovation Day and some of the teams that I've led, we've worked with Amazon Alexa, augmented reality, IoT, machine learning, computer vision and facial recognition. And one team that I led won the Think Different Innovation Award from Chick-fil-A for just thinking outside of the box.

Apart from that, we've recently opened a new Innovation Center in TechSquare, which is this huge technology hub in Midtown Atlanta. This is separate from our headquarters, and, there, we partner with universities like Georgia Tech to have year-round interns. We call the interns Innovators. We work with them to use emerging technologies and AI to solve business challenges. So we have a strong culture of innovation. I was lucky enough to be involved with the opening of the Innovation Center, and there are a lot of smart students out there.

Q. In your pursuit of AI and innovation, I am sure you work with many companies in the software industry. Are you finding is there anything that you need that is difficult for the industry to provide? Do they meet your requirements, especially for AI, or are there things that you could use that you're not finding from the software industry?

A. Before the advent of cloud services like Amazon Web Services, I would've said, yes, there's a lot lacking in the industry as far as support for AI. But now, thanks to AWS services like Amazon Machine Learning, Amazon Rekognition, which is their computer vision service, and Amazon Alexa Skills Kit, we're now able to quickly build prototypes to help prove out the feasibility of our innovative ideas.

And Amazon has also recently introduced SageMaker for advanced machine learning algorithms. Also there's a new product called DeepLens, which I can't wait to start playing around with, that allows for running deep learning models locally on a camera and to analyze and take actions on what it sees. There are so many opportunities to provide innovative solutions to the industry thanks to services like AWS.

Q. That sounds like a big recent change. We have written about a talent gap between the AI expertise that companies need from the employees or new hires, versus what is available on the market at a cost that companies can afford. Are you able to find the IT staff you need to support your efforts?

A. At Chick-fil-A, we typically look within and train within to find this talent and AI expertise. So Chick-fil-A hires really smart people that are just overall great software engineers. They're able to learn new things quickly. We all have a desire to innovate and a passion for technology, so we look within.

Q. So you avoid that whole issue of salary competition.

A. Right, we haven't run into that.

Q. Do you have any concerns about issues relating to the increased use of AI technology, such as privacy concerns or data bias? Are there any that you have to be aware of?

A. Personally, I am definitely concerned with bias, data bias and machine bias. I speak a lot about this topic at technical conferences. I always go back to the classic examples like the Google AI program that classified a few African Americans as gorillas instead of humans, or the computer vision program that couldn't even see African Americans. To me, that speaks to a lack of diversity in the data used to train the AI program. I believe that our reliance on

AI, which is just going to continue to grow, makes a very strong case for the need for diversity in technology. We should build systems without bias.

In my spare time outside of work at Chick-fil-A, just because I wanted to learn more about machine learning, I created a predictive policing machine learning algorithm called SAM, which stands for Suspicious Activity Monitor. SAM looks at a particular situation using computer vision, and predicts the likelihood of crime using machine learning. SAM looks at several attributes about the person and their current location in order to make a crime prediction, so just think pre-crime from [2002 film] "Minority Report."

When I created SAM, I intentionally excluded race as an attribute he considers because I didn't want him accused of racial profiling. So, you know, another programmer may not have considered this, but just that decision to exclude race, for me, was an aha moment because it showed that machine learning can actually, if we use it correctly, remove human bias from certain situations

When I switch gears and go back to Chick-fil-A and our use of AI, you know, in our industry, we pride ourselves on having outstanding customer service, which allows us to form emotional connections with our customers. If we start to rely too heavily on AI, that human element may diminish, which would really have an overall negative effect. So we just have to keep that in mind as we start to rely more on AI, that we always want to have that human element so that we can form strong emotional connections with our customers.

Q. Is there anything you would like to add or emphasize?

A. I would like to put in a plug for a recently-released AWS machine learning course I created with Manning Publications. Using interactive liveVideo, this is a crash course in using Amazon Web Services for machine learning, teaching you how to build a fully-working predictive algorithm.

Chapter 14: Executive Interview: Dany De Grave, Sanofi

Implementing AI projects company-wide;
Challenges include making data sets complete and useful,
Managing expectations, communicating results

Dany De Grave is Senior Director Science & Innovation, FluNXT, formerly Innovation Programs & External Networks, for the Pasteur Division of Sanofi, a French multinational biopharmaceutical company. He was also project leader for the Cognitive Computing for Regulatory Intelligence AI effort for the Information Technologies & Services department at Sanofi. He has held past positions at GlaxoSmithKline Biologicals, and SmithKline Beecham Biologicals. He recently spent a few minutes talking with AI Trends Editor John P. Desmond.

Q. What is your role at Sanofi and how would you describe the company?

A. As Senior Director of Innovation Programs and External Networks, my goal was to bring innovation into the company of a type that was so advanced that it allowed us to fundamentally change the way we work, to do things we couldn't do before. Also, it needed to be implemented economically and advance our current and upcoming projects. So, it needed to be 'cutting edge' innovation but not something that would be great only 20 years from now.

Sanofi is a diversified global healthcare company, present in more than 170 countries and providing a range of healthcare solutions to people, as our focus is exclusively people. We have a division focusing on diabetes and cardiovascular disease, a consumer healthcare division, a division focusing on specialty care, and also established medicines and emerging markets. The fifth focus area is called Sanofi Pasteur and is all about vaccines. It goes back to the days of Louis Pasteur, the French biologist who invented the principles of vaccination, and that's the area where I have been spending most of my activity for Sanofi. The global Sanofi organization has over 100,000 employees. It's quite an extensive operation.

Q. How does AI play into your role there?

A. When we started with AI a couple of years ago, AI fitted the definition of 'cutting-edge' innovation.

One of our first goals was to demonstrate that AI could be used in our field, that it really could change the way we work for the better. Since then, a lot of my work has been about leading the implementation of several AI projects across different Sanofi divisions in North America.

The types of projects are diverse, ranging from Research to late-stage development, and regulatory. Availability of data sources can come from either our own internal projects or through external sources. We work with people internally and with external partners. It has been quite a varied journey so far.

Q. What areas of AI innovation is Sanofi exploring these days?

A. Some groups might be actively exploring AI and some groups have already fully integrated AI into the way they work. In R&D, we have projects in biomarkers and genomics. We are exploring AI in applications for clinical development, marketing, regulatory, and manufacturing. There is not one big focus area; it is really about looking at how we operate and how can AI contribute or not.

Q. Can you say what AI technologies or approaches are being tried? What would you describe as the AI technology or approach primarily that's being used?

A. It entirely depends on the business case. If we are researching text as a data source, we need to use natural language processing (NLP). Some projects will combine both text and numbers as data sources. We try to find the best people to work with the algorithms suited for each project. There is not one standard approach.

Q. How far along is Sanofi in the adoption of AI, in your opinion?

A. AI is clearly part of a path forward. We are past the stage of wondering if AI will be useful, which was the case several years ago. The adoption of AI is now spreading across the different departments, divisions, and disciplines. It is at a stage where we are starting to explore in some areas while other departments have finished, completed projects. We have been doing work with external partners, while at the same time, we have hired data scientists and technical AI experts to do work in-house. A balanced approach is necessary to grow AI within the company by doing projects with both internal and external resources.

Q. Can you mention one or more outside partners you collaborate with in your pursuit of AI?

A. We have worked with Berg Health, Exscientia, and others. It has been a rich good series of interactions with a diverse group of external partners.

Q. Can you talk about any internal projects that may have been completed or implemented?

A. Sanofi is using AI to learn about how people respond to vaccines, so we're looking for biomarkers. We want to better understand what's happening at the time of vaccination and over time. What are the determinants of immune response to vaccination, and how could they be leveraged?

Another example is using AI in the regulatory domain. Sanofi is exploring the use of AI to understand the available regulatory information and to add a chatbot-type interaction with the information. That would enable us to ask a very specific regulatory-oriented question in a natural communication interface and receive an answer from the system. Instead of having people search through documents with different tools, we can have just one tool that gives us the answer and enables us to learn more.

Q. What would you say are the challenges in the adoption of AI at Sanofi? For example, how do you manage expectation?

A. AI is an emerging technology and that comes with its typical challenges. One challenge is access to data. Do we have the right data sets? Are the data sets complete or fragmented? Can we utilize them? Can we easily access them? Sometimes we have a lot of data, but we might not be able to use it because it may be that we don't have the appropriate clinical trial authorization due to consent. It complicates a little bit how things go. It is not just push the button and we're up and running. A lot needs to be verified.

Then there is also what I would call the human aspect. AI is a new technology. It is something that's going to create change. It is changing the way we operate and the way we think. As usual, there will be some early adopters and there will be those who first want to see lots of proof that AI can make a difference for their world; that AI can be a big help in their role.

As for managing expectations, it is easy to be impressed by those latest AI announcements from Google and others, showing all the wonderful things that AI can do and is doing; it is really impressive. What is very often not mentioned is that a lot of time, money, and effort have gone into these systems before they can generate those wonderful results.

A lot of work is needed to get these systems to do analyses in two weeks or in six weeks, or longer. Managing expectations is a bit of telling people it's not going to happen in the next couple of weeks. It is important to educate people on what we learn as we do AI projects, and what other people are learning around AI projects.

In our industry, with regulatory limitations on which data you can use for which type of analyses, it is a part of AI activities that requires effort and validation. It is a constraint some industries may not have. Also not much talked about is that with AI projects very often results only come at the end. That is after the system has been created and people have trained it. That takes time. Many people are not used to having to wait.

We have been living in a world that's more linear. We try experiments, we get results, we integrate them, we think about it. People see a continuous string of results. With AI, it can take some time before the system is up and running, trained, and then the results come along. Sometimes people start to get worried that the project is not going to end well because they don't see results. So that expectation needs to be managed.

Q. How does AI affect job titles and reporting paths in the organization?

A. I would call it a work in progress. It is emerging technology, so things change and companies will adapt. New job titles are being created, and new organizational structures are coming into effect, with AI as a key in those activities. This is all not happening overnight. This is a gradual, natural evolution for the organization.

Q. Are you able to find the people you need to carry out the work involving AI at Sanofi?

A. Yes, we are in an environment where we can attract people who want to use their AI talent to advance medicine to help develop life-saving products, and to overall contribute to making people's lives better. This has helped us to attract the right people to do AI work internally or to collaborate with externally. Also, many of our company sites are located very close to AI talent, so that certainly also helps.

Q. Do you have any advice for young people interested in a career in AI, for what education and experience they should pursue?

A. Besides the technical side of things, which is very important, advice I would give to young people entering this domain is to make sure they develop good communication skills. It is something not really talked about, but we have people on AI projects from different disciplines: AI experts, scientists, and business people. They all speak kind of a different language, even if they all speak English.

So whatever domain you choose to go into, machine learning or natural language processing, for example, it's important to be able to translate your results into a message understandable by the other people involved. I have seen it happen, and the risk is real, that the AI project otherwise will be perceived as failed or not living up to its high expectations, when it actually has very useful results. Only due to a communication style not well adapted to the audience.

That is a shame when you have done something great, but the translation is not there, so it's not understood by other people. That is to no one's advantage. It certainly doesn't help the scientist when they do not fully understand what is coming out of the analysis. And the businessperson will not be able to take it further to make good use out of it. Our work is to provide healthcare solutions to people and to help our patients. AI is a tool. If it cannot be translated across the organization, it's not very useful.

Q. Is there anything you would like to add?

A. AI is here and it's not going to go away, but we still need a lot of effort to really make the best use of it. Organizations will have to further evolve, people will have to start using it in their thinking, and in the way they work. The output of AI puts us a little bit on a different path. So, there's more work to do and more skills to be developed.

Learn more at Sanofi.

Chapter 15: Executive Interview: Yoshua Bengio

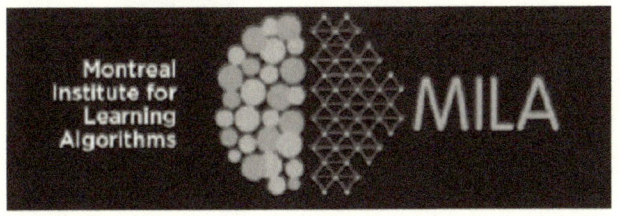

**Combining AI Research,
Business Collaboration,
Thoughts on Impact of AI on Society**

Yoshua Bengio is among the most cited Canadian computer scientists. He is the author of two books and more than 200 publications, the most cited being in the areas of deep learning, recurrent neural networks, probabilistic learning algorithms, natural language processing and manifold learning.

He earned a PhD in Computer Science from McGill University in 1991 and worked at the Canadian Institute for Advanced Research (CIFAR)

Yoshua Bengio of MILA, University of Montreal alongside Yann LeCun (now at Facebook) and Geoffrey Hinton (now at Google). He has collaborated with IBM in work on the Watson supercomputer.

His current interests are centered around a quest for AI through machine learning, and include fundamental questions on deep learning and representation learning, the geometry of generalization in high-dimensional spaces, manifold learning, biologically inspired learning algorithms, and challenging applications of statistical machine learning. He recently participated in an interview with journalists learning about Canada's AI initiative that included Eliot Weinman, Executive Editor of AI Trends.

Q. Why is it important for the Canadian government to engage in this AI initiative?

A. AI is not just another technology. It will have a big impact on our societies, and there are many ethical and social questions associated with how AI is being deployed and how it will be deployed. If we don't think about these considerations, the public will eventually reject advanced technologies that they see as threatening and against their well-being. So governments have to really care about these questions, whether for moral reasons or for practical reasons.

Q. What would be your AI horror scenario?

A. I am most concerned about the use of AI in the military and security arenas. I'm sure you've heard about killer robots, and you may have also heard of how the technology can be used to recognize people from their facial images. So there are Big Brother scenarios that could be upon us if we're not careful. I also have concerns related to privacy issues when we are dealing with private data. Then we have economic issues. Automation will be accelerated with AI; that may create more inequality than we already suffer. And that is at the level of people, companies and countries. To have more countries involved will create a healthier playing field.

Q. What is the role of universities in the evolution of AI?

A. I am a professor at University of Montreal; we have created MILA (Montreal Institute for Learning Algorithms), which is similar to the Vector Institute (collaboration of government and business in partnership with University of Toronto) which has similar goals and were both funded by the federal government and the provincial government. These institutes - there's another in Alberta (Alberta

Machine Intelligence Institute) - have been set up so they will have more agility than universities have, but they're still academic research organizations. They also have a mandate to help the ecosystem through the startups and companies that are creating value with AI.

These institutes are in a better position to be neutral about how AI will be used and keep in mind the well-being of people, and to orient research in directions that will be good for people, and engage in the public dialogue in a credible way. I think it's good that companies like Facebook and Google participate in that dialogue, but I'm not sure if they are neutral agents in those discussions. Universities, which care, first and foremost, about the public good, are really important agents in the discussions and in the kind of research that can be done.

Q. What steps can government take to foster this dialogue?

A. Here in Montreal, we are creating an organization that will be focused on the social, economic and ethical questions around AI. It will sponsor research in the social sciences and humanities around AI, but also will participate in the public debate. I think we don't have all the answers to how to do this right. Scholars and scientists need to really think through this and engage the public. We did something like this in the last six months in Montreal and in Quebec, and also in Ontario. After a forum of experts, we brought in ordinary people. We went to public libraries and places where people could comment and discuss the questions. We're coming up with something that will be initiated by scholars and experts, and also have feedback and contributions from ordinary people. I think we have to continue in that direction.

This observatory on AI will be in a good position to make recommendations to governments, which will be part of the mission both locally and in different countries. The questions are pretty much the same in most countries. I think there should be a global coordination about these questions. There are issues like military use which will obviously need to be international, and even questions about regulating companies, which are multinationals. It would be much better if we can agree on principles globally.

Q. What do you see as the next evolution of the core technology that enables what we know of as AI today?

A. I'm a scientist. I don't have a crystal ball. And I can make educated guesses like many people. But one thing for sure is that there are obstacles on our way towards smarter machines, and it's always been like this when we make progress. We've achieved something important, and now we see that there are other challenges. We've made huge progress in industry using supervised learning where humans have to really teach machines by telling them what to do. A lot of the current emphasis in basic research is on supervised learning or reinforcement learning, where the machines have to learn in a more autonomous way. And we haven't solved that in a satisfactory way yet. It will probably take years, or decades to really make big breakthroughs there. But given the exponential growth of research in these areas, I'm very optimistic that things will move very swiftly.

Q. Are you concerned that the massive investments in AI today are too risky?

A. One reason why companies are investing so much, and are so optimistic, is that a lot of future wealth growth from AI doesn't depend on new discoveries. In other words, we take what we have already scientifically, and we just make a lot of progress in the hardware. That's going to happen. It's moving. We will make progress in bringing together the right data. Like medical data, we don't do a good job yet. In lots of industries and sectors, the ingredients for applying that science are not there yet, but they will be there soon.

We have at least a decade to just reap the benefits of the science we already have. On top of that, there's so much money being poured into research, both in industry and in academia, that it would be surprising if the science doesn't move forward over the next decade. So it's almost a sure gain. Now, of course, you know, commercial enterprises can fail for all kinds of reason. But at a high level, I think it's a very safe bet.

Q. Is China ahead in the race to be the leading AI country?

A. I don't like to make like these kinds of comparisons. Silicon Valley is a very small place. The progress can come from anywhere in the world. China does have huge advantages in this race. One of the most important ones is that it's the biggest market in the world, and has the volumes of data that go with that. So from the point of view of investing, this is a very appealing place to do AI. And in addition, there's a huge enthusiasm for AI in China from all quarters. And lots and lots of students are jumping into this. It's a worldwide phenomenon, but I think with all the enthusiasm behind it, China probably wins the race for now.

Q. Do you see big companies and startups and small companies collaborating to advance AI?

A. There is room for many kinds of business models in this new world. Large companies have leadership strong enough to make the fast turns that are needed, and companies like Element AI can help with that that. And big companies will be in competition with up and running small companies, building new products and new services which may not even exist now. New markets will be created. I'm also a big believer in the collaboration between startups and large companies. They have complimentary advantages. This is important from the point of view of a country with a national strategy because the startups are more agile. They can more easily recruit people who are excited about the fast pace of development. They can recruit talent more easily.

But the large companies have the larger market where they can deploy. They have lots of cash to invest, and they have lots of data. Ideally companies, a little bit like researchers, learn to cooperate better with their strengths and weaknesses to build something stronger.

Q. Are you concerned about the risk of jobs lost to AI automation?

A. Absolutely. The potential impact on the job market is very serious. It's not going to happen in one day, but it will happen way too fast for our ability to handle those changes. Many people are likely to lose their jobs in the middle of their careers.

We have to rethink our social safety net. Most developed countries have a social safety net, but it's been designed for a particular kind of economy. We will need to look into things like a universal basic income, and do more pilots. We may have to forget about our traditional values around work, such as if you don't work, you don't get money. And that's only one aspect of it. We need to rethink the education system so people can be rescaled in the middle of their career, while they are at a job.

The education system will need to train people in a way that is more appropriate for a fast-changing world, where human skills are going to be more important than they were in the past. Of course, we want to train more scientists and engineers; that's a no-brainer. But we have to train people not for one job that's very, very specialized, but rather how to think for themselves about how to be good citizens, and to rapidly learn the skills they need.

And we have to ask what is going to be the impact on society? Will AI be beneficial for the whole society or just a few people? I don't have the answers but I think it's important to ask the questions and let the market by themselves figure out the answers. Those answers might not be in favor of ordinary people. Governments need to think about this and if necessary, find the right regulations.

Q. How is MILA progressing and can you describe your typical day?

A. MILA is the Montreal Institute for Learning Algorithms, a machine learning research lab with business collaboration as part of the mission. It's growing very fast. It already has the highest concentration of deep learning researchers in academia in the world. We're going to be doubling the number of professors over the next few years, thanks to the Canadian government.

MILA is mostly academic in nature, a non-profit, but with the mandate to help companies, to guide them in their development of AI.

I love working at the university. It allows me to be a more neutral agent in the changes that are coming, and gives me a voice that can have an impact as we adapt to this changing world of AI. Also, I'm in a position to steer research in directions that I think are important, and to contribute to the training of the next generation. I think this is something really, really important. I just enjoy the research with all of my students, which I would lose if I went to private industry.

Learn more at [MILA.](MILA)

Chapter 16: Executive Interview: Amir Banifatemin

**Driving AI Innovation: New Services, Investment
and Societal Good are Goals of XPRIZE Competition**

"The question that everyone needs to ask themselves is, while we are building new innovative approaches with AI, how could we also think about bringing value to society?" - Amir Banifatemi

Amir Banifatemi is the Prize Lead of the IBM Watson AI XPRIZE; he has more than 25 years of experience in development and growth of emerging and transformative technologies. XPRIZE is a global leader in designing and implementing innovative competition models that aim to solve the world's greatest challenges and to encourage technological development to benefit humanity.

Mr. Banifatemi began his career at the European Space Agency; he then held executive positions at Airbus, and the European Commission division for information society and media. He

Amir Banifatemi of IBM Watson AI XPRIZE

also has managed two venture capital funds and contributed to the formation of more than 10 startups with an emphasis on Predictive Technologies, IoT, and Healthcare. He is a guest lecturer and an adjunct MBA professor at UC Berkeley, Chapman University, Claremont McKenna College, UC Irvine, and HEC Paris.

He recently spoke with AI Trends editor John P. Desmond.

Q. How would you describe the big picture mission of XPRIZE?

XPRIZE, basically, is an innovation engine. We find opportunities for radical transformation of society through incentivized participation of the crowd. So we leverage exponential technologies, which are the most advanced technologies, deep technologies such as artificial intelligence, blockchain, quantum computing, genetic engineering, IoT sensors, 3D printing and so on. We seek to enable breakthroughs and exponential progress of those. We are preparing society for the future by trying to identify leveraged ways to bring radical innovation to everyone.

Q.Is that what the leverage is, the prize?

Many factors come into play when you talk to teams about motivation for being a part of the XPRIZE competition. Teams say that the ecosystem, resources available and competitive spirit are front of mind - all of these drive investment into the challenge area. In many cases, the prize does factor into the equation. In certain areas, for instance, government spending might not be enough or there is no incentive for governments to spend resources, or when venture capital is not investing into certain areas, or research has not been progressing. One way to look at an XPRIZE is an opportunity to accelerate and find teams to work on those topics that have not made progress or are not going to make progress in a reasonable amount of time.

The same thing that happened about almost 100 years ago, when the first commercial aviation began. A prize of $25,000 incentivized people to travel by air from New York to Paris. Charles Lindbergh won that prize and that opened up the whole aviation industry. The number of people trying to be creative and innovative about aviation -- engines, everything -- went through the roof so that opened up the whole aviation industry at that time.

And the same way, today, we can say that in 2003 with SpaceShipOne winning the $10 million prize to incentivize engineers to create a craft that would transport a three-person crew 100 kilometers into the atmosphere. That was really the beginning of commercial space travel. Virgin Galactic purchased the license of that and started Virgin Galactic. A number of startups and research then spun out and the whole space industry opened up. And, today, you see how many people are trying to go to space, to go to Mars, to explore other planets. That was basically the opening.

So what we're saying about leverage is that when we open up an opportunity to a number of teams with a very strong innovation challenge and people respond positively to that challenge, then a number of innovations happen and unlikely teams get created. Because many, many people may have opportunities and ideas about solving a problem who may not come forward, necessarily. So we create an incentive.

Q. XPRIZE in December announced 59 teams advancing in the $5 million dollar competition for the Watson IBM Watson AI XPRIZE, which is a four-year global competition. Where are you now on that schedule?

The global competition started in June of 2016. We invited teams to come and compete for that prize, sponsored by IBM. Meaning, that the purse is given by IBM for the winners, therefore the name of IBM Watson on the prize. And at that time, about 10,000 requests came through; 800 teams got started. Out of those 800 teams, 150 teams got an approval by the judges to start the competition because they demonstrated the needed capabilities. The competition is a four-year competition with different milestones.

The first milestone is year one, where we go from round one to round two. And to go to round two, teams have to demonstrate that they're working on meaningful projects and they are tackling the guidelines of the competition. So 59 teams out of the 150 demonstrated that, so these 59 that we announced in December. Now we are going into the second year, engaging in solution development. At the end of 2018, the teams will submit their work for judges to review and decide who is going to round three. Round four will be the semi-final; the finalists will be on the TED stage in 2020. So this stepping stone to a prize is usually the way an

XPRIZE functions. It's always a longer process. It's not a three- or six-month effort. And, today, teams are gradually engaging into their solution development, now.

Q. In your release, you announced the top 10 teams. Could you comment on what you're seeing from these AI innovators?

Yes. It doesn't mean that these teams are going to win. It means that at this phase, on round one, these are the teams that demonstrated more advancement and have put more work into the competition. The domains in which they are working include health and wellness, civil society, space and frontiers, learning and human potential, shelter, energy, and planet and environment.

So these teams are actually working on very specific problems related, for instance, to managing depression, or helping with democracy, or helping with improving the environment and clean water. Some of the 59 teams are tackling problems in the same domain, but they definitely have different focuses and the type of AI and technology they're using is very varied. We may not have full knowledge of what they're doing yet. We have validated that they're working on something meaningful, which has impact attached to it and they have demonstrated that they know what they're talking about and they have the technical abilities to deliver. What they're actually going to be delivering, we will see in the next coming months because they're actually building it.

Q. How do you characterize the entrants? Are they practitioners in the field who are working in business? Or are they students or both? Or is all types?

We have actually a good mix of teams created with individuals coming from academia, from research, from corporations; most of them are startups. There are a few students but not many. Teams have to be multidisciplinary because to tackle AI for impact, you have to tackle both -- AI and impact. So if you're talking about a project such as improving enterprise quality control, for instance, you need to know something about quality control and you need to know something about AI. So for that reason, teams are usually multidisciplinary, have both sides, the AI side and the AI/machine learning and everything that's related to AI but also the domain, the expertise of the domain. So those teams are not just teams of students, or just a team of academics, or just a team of corporate people, or just a team of business people. These are very much mixed teams.

Q. What is the best use of AI for the most impact?

I'm trying to bring attention to the fact that AI can used for the most immediate and pressing issues that society faces. Whether that issue is unemployment or economic output or healthcare or education. And corporations have to be imaginative and modern in creating new products and more wealth and more jobs. Every now and then, some technologies come forward and give us the opportunity to think better about applications built with them. Machine learning and artificial intelligence give us more power to predict, to analyze, to understand, and to create more automation and to learn more with data. So we ask how can we employ these capabilities to problems that are definitely more important to tackle, such as for everyone to have a better life, to have better welfare, to participate more in democracy and to basically have better skills and to be employable and so forth. This is how we look at impact.

The question that everyone needs to ask themselves is, while we are building new innovative approaches with AI, how could we also think about bringing value to society? So think of it as a corporation that makes money and profits and generates new value, and is also thinking about being sustainable, having less impact on the environment and helping better its employees and its community. So AI gives us the opportunity to ask a number of questions. Of course, artificial intelligence is built with algorithms, computing power, data. Most of the time it can be autonomous. Sometimes it cannot be autonomous, and it has to be used with human help. The amount of information that we inject into AI programs certainly contains our biases, and certainly exposes people to less privacy. How can we also be aware of those? So that question about impact brings a lot of other questions next to it, which I'm suggesting we should be aware of and think about.

Corporations have a role, definitely, to participate in this dialogue. And while they're pursuing reinvention of their businesses with AI, I think there's an opportunity, also, for them to understand the implications of AI through the whole company itself and the ecosystem in which they operate.

Q. What is the impact of AI on corporations reinventing themselves?

Today AI is set to transform all business in ways that we have not seen since the industrial revolution. So, really, we are in a new revolution. And, fundamentally, AI is helping business reinvent how they run, how they operate, how they compete, how they thrive, how they create value. So if, for instance, technologies help to lower costs and create new jobs or create new growth opportunities -- this is how AI is basically helping enterprises reinvent themselves.

Maybe the type of jobs and skills they need to incorporate is going to be different. Maybe the training of employees has to happen sooner, maybe lowering costs and increasing productivity helps us generate better profits that could be repurposed to other areas. Maybe some aspect of jobs will be lost and then can be converted into something else. This can help not only enterprises, but it also helps governments, nonprofits, and the society as a whole. And I think the understanding of that topic is critical. So the impact of AI on corporations is really the opportunity to think again about, one, how can we create value? And second, how can the tools of productivity and growth play out, again, with AI as an ingredient?

Many people say that AI will boost profit and innovation. Some people say that AI will lead responsiveness. Some people think that AI is going to bring more inclusion. Some people think that AI will increase automation so that jobs will be lost. All of these are interesting to consider. The impact is going to be central to each organization to decide upon and take action. And I think that opportunity, again, the same way it was important for society, it's important for enterprises because it's part of the core of creating jobs and value and wealth. And because products and service are fundamental to the growth of enterprises, AI is definitely a conversation to have. I think all big knowledge partners, consultancies -- everyone basically says the same thing about AI helping enterprises reinvent themselves today.

Q. What would you say to people who fear AI?

For many people, AI is unknown. Many uses of AI are flying somewhat under the radar for most people. We've seen AI used for dramatic effect, and for some, the knowledge of AI comes, mostly, from science fiction and media portraying AI always in the form of a Terminator or dystopian face or dystopian scenario. AI in the real world is different. AI is, as a core, is a set of technologies that help us automate certain things. Automation will probably make our life better. Automation will help us do things stronger, better, faster, in a larger scale.

And any new tool probably creates a number of fears and the fear of unemployment is probably the number one fear today. However AI is allowing us to create new jobs as well. The fear of losing privacy and being observed is a second fear. I personally don't subscribe to those fears as long as, we, as a society, as a group, as a collective, take actions to make sure that AI is built in a beneficial way.

AI creates new ways for us to reboot everything and think about it and talk about it. But I don't transfer that into fear. I transfer that into a responsibility that we have to ask those hard questions and make sure that we have good boundaries around that and good checks and balances and make sure that AI is, first, beneficial and built safely. And, second, that we use AI for the right reasons and we don't put it everywhere and that we have some responsibility and some third-party check-in's and so forth.

Q. Are there key areas of AI where you're seeing innovation today?

AI is advancing very fast in certain areas, such as healthcare, which has seen tremendous benefits. Imagine cognition disease diagnostics, assisting doctors with robotics, assisting with some medical therapeutic acts and, basically, planning in general of healthcare issues. But, also, in education, where personalized learning is becoming more important. You can have more interactions, you can incorporate automation, in terms of certain types of experiences in learning. And AI is helping with climate and weather and water management, so climate and environment is getting benefits from it. Of course, everyone sees self-driving cars as automation happening on the road, where we can now detect objects and manage the car movement at a certain level. Today, we're not at full capacity of level five autonomous driving but we are close to level three. And teams and labs and corporations are working on improving that. These are the low-hanging areas where we see immediate application but corporations, government, everyone is looking at AI in everything -- from economic participation, to democracy, to helping psychology issues or helping committees connect better -- we've seen so many examples just with this competition. But this competition represents only a tiny, a very tiny fraction of all the ideas and possibilities that many people are working on today.

Q. What message should readers of AI Trends take away?

Well first, and foremost, I think it's important that everyone one of us understands better what AI is and is not. And understand what it can do and try to participate in dialogue and conversations around privacy, ethics and governance of AI. Test products, give feedback, and participate with groups and teams that are working on hard topics and are trying to collaborate and collectively make sure that AI is well-understood. It's a real change and I think participating, understanding, and discussing it and sharing the right facts and data is important. Today we have opportunities to showcase practical applications that benefit everyone. Let's identify those and push those first to be implemented, for the majority of people to benefit and to create a better society. So I will say this is the first stage that we can focus on and we have a responsibility to focus on it.

Learn more at IBM Watson AI XPRIZE.

ABOUT THE AUTHOR

John P. Desmond is editor of the AI Trends newsletter published by Cambridge Innovation Institute and supporting the AI World Conference & Expo, founded and produced by Eliot Weinman. John has been a technology journalist for many years, with a content focus primarily on software development, having worked for many publishing entrepreneurs.

John also works today as a teacher of high school students dealing with anxiety and depression in a psychiatric hospital setting. He also consults on transportation for a public school collaborative, and writes about entrepreneurs in the technical marine economy on Cape Cod.

For more information, visit
www.jdcontentservices.com.

www.ingramcontent.com/pod-product-compliance
Lightning Source LLC
Chambersburg PA
CBHW020647220526
45464CB00001B/328